The Warren Legacy
What the Paranormal Reveals About Consciousness and Reality

CHRIS MCKINNELL

Director, Warren Legacy Foundation for Paranormal Research
Grandson of Ed and Lorraine Warren

ISBN: 979-8-9956167-0-2

DEDICATION

To my grandmother and grandfather, Lorraine and Ed Warren For your

guidance, unwavering love, and fearless dedication to
helping others.

For the example of selflessness and compassion you set, showing me that
true strength lies not in power, but in service.

For teaching me to seek truth beyond fear, to trust in my path, and to
never stop questioning.

Everything in these pages began with you.

With love and gratitude, Chris

CONTENTS

	Acknowledgements	5
	Foreword	7
	Preface	10
I.	The Education Of Fear	11
II.	The Truth Underneath	25
III.	The Farmer	31
IV.	What We Actually Are	36
V.	The Witness	42
VI.	The Evidence	56
VII.	The City of The Dead	62
VIII.	How We Access What Lies Beyond	68
IX.	Annabelle Comes Home	83
X.	Manifesting Reality	90
XI.	The Tapestry	101
XII.	The Chess Board	109
XIII.	Alpha and Omega	117
XIV.	Why Bother	123
XV.	The Gift That Is Death	128
XVI.	The Ocean In A Drop	134
XVII.	Addendum One: Public Thesis, An Accessible Introduction To The Scientific Ideas Behind This Book	141
XVIII.	Addendum Two: Practical Guidance For The Frightened And The Curious	170
XIX.	Addendum Three: A Guide For The Gifted	181
XX.	Glossary	189
XX1.	Bibliography	220

ACKNOWLEDGMENTS

This book would not be possible without the extraordinary work of the amazing researchers of The Warren Legacy Foundation for Paranormal Research and especially the help of my friend Mark Robson in ensuring that the book reached the public.

Bless you all.

THE WARREN LEGACY FOUNDATION FOR PARANORMAL RESEARCH

FOREWORD

By Mark Robson
Founder of East Durham Paranormal Research Group

I was eleven years old when the course of my life quietly changed direction. It was an ordinary evening in the North-East of England, and I was sitting in front of the television when a BBC show about Borley Rectory drew me in and refused to let me go. Most children that age were probably thinking about football or friends. I was transfixed by a building in Essex that had been called the most haunted house in England, by the stories of unexplained phenomena that had unsettled everyone who had ever crossed its threshold, and by the very real possibility that the world was a great deal stranger and more remarkable than I had been led to believe.

That single evening set something in motion that has never stopped. The interest that Borley sparked, led me over the years that followed, to read everything I could find on paranormal investigation, on the nature of hauntings, on the people who dedicated their lives to understanding what so many others simply chose to dismiss. It was through that reading, and through the cases that shaped the field, that I came to Ed and Lorraine Warren. What struck me most was not the dramatic nature of the cases they investigated, though those were remarkable enough. It was the unwavering conviction that ran through everything they did: that people in need deserved to be helped, respectfully, compassionately and without judgement.

The Warren Legacy means something different to everyone who encounters it, and I think that is precisely as it should be. For some it represents a body of casework spanning decades, a reference point for some of the most significant paranormal investigations ever carried out. For others it is a philosophical framework, a way of approaching the unknown that holds together rigor and open-mindedness, scepticism and genuine curiosity. For me, the Warren Legacy has always been about something more personal than any single case or theory. It is about taking a framework, understanding it thoroughly, and then having the intellectual honesty to question it at every turn. It is about using that process of questioning not to undermine what has come before, but to build something of your own that can serve the people who need you.

That is why the work of the Warren Legacy Foundation for Paranormal Research matters so much. We live in a world that is more connected than ever before, where people from every background, every faith and every set of beliefs can find themselves experiencing something they do not understand, something that frightens them or that shakes their sense of what is real. The Foundation exists as a bridge across all of that difference, a place where a family in the United States, a couple in the United Kingdom, or anyone else anywhere in the world can reach out and know that they will be heard. Not judged. Not dismissed. Not asked to conform to someone else's theology or worldview before they receive help. Simply heard and helped.

Ed and Lorraine Warren understood this at a level that I continue to find extraordinary. Whatever one thinks about any individual case or conclusion, what cannot be disputed is the consistency of their motivation. They helped people. They showed up when they were needed, often at considerable personal cost, and they did so because they believed that helping those in distress was not merely a professional obligation but a moral one. That principle is the most important thing they left behind, more important than any investigation, any book or any film. It is the heart of the legacy that Chris McKinnell has carried forward, and it is the principle that should guide everyone who works in this field.

At East Durham Paranormal Research Group, that principle is the foundation of everything we do. We approach each case with a blend of science, theory and healthy scepticism, because sound investigation demands nothing less. But technique and equipment are only ever the tools. The purpose beneath them is always the same: to help. We make no charge for what we do, we work without judgement, and we remain committed to following the evidence wherever it leads, even when it leads somewhere uncomfortable or unexpected. If that sounds familiar, it should. It is what Ed and Lorraine modelled, and what this book so clearly reflects.

The Warren Legacy: What the Paranormal Reveals About Consciousness and Reality is, on one level, a deeply personal book. Chris McKinnell writes from the inside of a remarkable family history, drawing on decades of investigation and a genuine lifetime of engagement with questions that most people find too difficult or too unsettling to sit with for long. But it is also a book with something important to say to anyone who has ever wondered what lies beyond our ordinary understanding of the world, whether they come to those questions through faith, through loss, through curiosity or through an eleven-year-old's memory of a television show they have never been quite able to forget.

Read this book with an open mind, question everything in it as you go, and let it prompt you to develop your own thinking rather than simply borrowing someone else's conclusions. That, more than anything, is what the Warren Legacy has taught me. Ask the question, do the work, and always, above everything else, be there for the people who need you.

PREFACE

Why are we here? Does life have any meaning, or is it just a series of random events leading to death? Is God real? Is any single religion correct? In a universe where NASA estimates billions of potentially habitable worlds exist, does anything I do really matter? What happens when we die?

The endless quest of my life has been to find answers to these questions. Given that I am the only grandson of Ed and Lorraine Warren, world-famous paranormal investigators, and that I started delving into the paranormal at sixteen, you might expect my understanding of reality came purely from investigating hauntings.

But the paranormal taught me something more profound: that consciousness survives death, that change is possible even after we die, and that if spirits can transform, so can we. That realization shaped everything that came after, more than four decades of field investigation and study across dozens of countries, learning disciplines as different as psychology, consciousness studies, and quantum physics, sitting with traditions most Americans will never encounter.

The paranormal opened the door. The journey through it gave me answers.

I. THE EDUCATION OF FEAR

It was the first week of August, 1981. A typical sweltering and humid day in New Hartford, Connecticut, when my grandfather Ed Warren called me with an unexpected and unwelcome request.

Chris, there's a poltergeist terrorizing a family in Lee, Massachusetts, and I want you to join me tonight.

I was sixteen years old and about to enter my last year of high school. Growing up with Ed and Lorraine Warren, world-famous ghost hunters, had left me terrified of the dark. I had spent my childhood shuffling between social workers and psychologists because of my extreme fear of what I sensed in the darkness. The idea of going into a haunted house where a family was being physically and spiritually abused was not something I had ever considered. Unfortunately, my grandfather had other ideas.

"Sure, Gramps, I replied automatically, but why do you want to take me?"

"Your grandmother can't join me this evening. I'm going to need your help. My assistant, Paul Bartz, will also be with us."

"I've only gone on lecture tours with you. I don't really know anything about this. How on earth can I help?"

My grandfather chuckled. "It's time for you to start learning."

We arranged a time early that evening, and I went to tell my mother what was going on. Judy is their only child and she has avoided the paranormal her entire life. It terrifies her, and she never wanted me or my sister to have anything to do with it. To my surprise, she seemed to have no problem with my joining my grandfather.

She gently suggested it might be good for me to face my fears.

She wasn't wrong. But she had no idea what she was sending me into.

At 7 PM my grandfather and Paul showed up, and I was on my way to what would become the most terrifying night of my life. Paul Bartz was a student activities director at the University of Connecticut who had been assisting my grandparents occasionally for the past few years, a young man with long blond hair and a friendly, easy-going nature. Just having him along put me at ease.

As the evening turned unseasonably cooler, on the forty-minute drive up to Lee on scenic old Route 8, my grandfather explained what he knew about the haunting.

Daniel and Liz Scout inherited their home from his uncle. He died several months ago, and they moved in with their two girls. The very first night, the couple were in their bed when the glowing white figure of a little boy appeared in their bedroom doorway and said, "Where do all the lonely people go?" Liz had converted from Judaism to marry her husband and was now a devout Catholic. She was terrified and contacted her priest the next morning to come and do a house blessing. After Father Scarpelli finished his blessing the child never returned. Unfortunately it was replaced by something much worse.

Gramps was always a natural storyteller. Daniel had found work at the local mill and was working rotating shifts. That night he was on third shift. Liz had put the girls to bed in their bedrooms across the hall. Just as she was settling in, a massive black figure appeared in her doorway, filling it completely. Liz had her rosary on the bed post and it reached over and picked it up, twirling it as if to say, "You think this is going to stop me?" She ran around the figure to her first daughters room directly across the hall. She tried to open it, but the door knob refused to turn. The pull-down stairs to the attic above her head came crashing down on her, knocking her senseless. The whole time the figure loomed ominously at her back. As she struggled to her feet, she managed to open the doors to each of the girls bedrooms and get them out of the house. They spent the night in the car, waiting for Daniel to come home from work.

Photographic evidence from the Lee, Massachusetts case, 1981. The dark figure visible here is consistent with what Chris McKinnell and others witnessed during their investigation that night. This was his first paranormal investigation, at age sixteen.

Over the next couple of weeks, the phenomena intensified. Kitchen cabinets would fly open and plates and glasses would be flung with tremendous force at the family. Tables and chairs, dressers and small appliances would rocket across the room. Daniel and Liz decided they could not stay there and moved in with his mother. That's when they contacted me.

I sat in the backseat, watching the Farmington River as we drove northward. I was terrified. But I also knew, somewhere beneath the terror, that I had been moving toward a night like this one for my entire life.

The Lee, Massachusetts case, 1981, Chris' first paranormal investigation at age sixteen. The case   that changed everything.

It started when I was three years old.

My grandparents kept a museum in their home in Monroe, Connecticut, a room filled with the artifacts from decades of investigation. Dolls. Masks. Statues. Objects that had been removed from cases because their presence alone was considered dangerous. I had wandered in there alone one evening and the door swung shut behind me. It was already getting dark outside. I couldn't get out. Ugly figurines stared at me from every surface. A tiger skin with its snarling head seemed poised to devour me. I stood in the middle of that room and screamed the way only a three-year-old can, until my grandfather heard me from his office in the back of the museum and came to rescue me.

He got me out in moments. But something stayed behind when I left that room. It followed me home and it slept with me every night for the next thirteen years.

Fear. A cold, specific, unreasonable fear of the dark. Of what moved in it. Of what I sensed at the edges of rooms that I could never see clearly enough to name.

Around the same time, I had a playmate named Charlie Brandt. His father Herbert was a mentor to my father, and Charlie and I were nearly the same age, thrown together the way young children are. We played together. He was just a boy. I had no way to know that a few years later, in 1971, Charlie would walk into the bathroom where his father was shaving and his mother was taking a bath, shoot his father, and murder his mother. That he would be institutionalized for a single year and then released. That his crimes would eventually claim at least twenty-nine more lives, ending only when he took his own.

I did not know any of that then. I only knew him as a child I played with, in the ordinary way of childhood. But I think about it now. I think about the fact that before I was old enough to read, I was already living inside two of the darkest truths this world contains, that some places hold something that does not wish us well, and that evil does not always announce itself. Sometimes it has a child's face and your fathers friends last name, and you would never know.

I grew up moving constantly. By the time I was eight we had lived in eight different homes. Every new bedroom was colder than the last, it seemed. I could hear things moving in the dark. I could feel presences at the edges of my perception, just beyond what the light could reach. My parents sent me to social workers and psychologists and none of them could explain it, because none of them knew what I was actually experiencing. My father didn't believe in the paranormal. My mother was terrified of it. And my grandmother Lorraine, who could have helped me more than anyone alive, was trying to preserve a family peace too fragile to survive the truth. So she stayed silent, and I stayed afraid, and I slept with the light on every single night.

What I didn't know then, what I couldn't have understood, was that I wasn't imagining things.

I was perceiving them.

There is a difference. I would spend years learning to understand it.

The first time I began to grasp that difference, I was fourteen years old.

I had been traveling on a lecture tour with my grandparents, one of the few things that bridged the fractures in our family, when a television crew from PM Magazine joined us somewhere in Ohio or Missouri. After several hours of interviews in a hotel lobby, they brought us to a house with a reported haunting. We were not allowed inside. We stood on the street in front of it.

A local newspaper reporter stood beside me. He had been preparing a story on the case and had his notes in hand, the family's account of what they had experienced, documented before we arrived. He had not yet published it. He had not shared it with anyone.

My grandmother stood in front of that house and began to speak.

An apparition of a large man with a bloody apron. The smell of rotting flesh rising from the kitchen. Specific incidents the family had reported in their own words.

I was standing next to the reporter. As my grandmother spoke, I was watching his notes. Detail by detail, she described what was written in front of him, things she had never been told, from a house she had never entered, confirmed by documentation that existed before she opened her mouth.

I watched the reporters face change.

I understood something in that moment that I have never been able to unfeel. Whatever my grandmother was doing, it was real. Whatever she was perceiving, it was there. And if she could perceive it, then what

I had been sensing in dark rooms my entire childhood was not fear playing tricks on my mind. It was information I didn't yet know how to read.

That was the beginning of a question I would spend the rest of my life trying to answer.

Two years passed. I turned sixteen. I had a beat-up old car with bald tires and I drove it on dark country roads in the rain as though I were invincible, the way sixteen-year-olds do.

One night that summer I was driving home from a party through rain-slicked roads that were pitch black, when I glanced into my rearview mirror.

There was an old man sitting in the back seat.

I spun around immediately. No one was there. I turned on the overhead light, checked every corner of the car, and drove home as fast as those bald tires would carry me.

The next morning I went to work at the Canton Bakeshop. And out of the corner of my eye, I kept seeing an old man watching me. Not clearly. Not directly. Always at the edge of my vision. Always gone when I turned to look. I was more confused than frightened. I didn't understand what was happening or why this particular face kept appearing.

About a week later I mentioned it to my mother. She went to the cupboard and pulled out the family photo album. She found a photograph and held it up.

"Is this him?" she asked. "Yes. Who is he?"

She told me it was her grandfather. Jim Moran. Lorraine's father. He had died when I was four years old. She had been worried about me that night, my terrible car, the rain, the dark roads, and she had prayed to him to watch over me.

Georgiana and James Moran, the parents of Lorraine Warren. Jim Moran, described by all who knew him as a warm and devoted man, appeared to Chris McKinnell in a rearview mirror on a rainy night in 1981, answering his mother's prayer for his safety.

He had always been devoted to me as a small child. By all accounts a warm and gentle man who would steal me away for entire days, taking me to meet his friends, bragging about how intelligent I was to anyone who would listen. I had no memory of him. I was too young when he died. But he apparently remembered me.

The evidence was specific. I described someone I had no conscious memory of ever meeting. My mother confirmed the identification from a photograph. The description matched. The timing, the very night she had prayed, matched.

Love, it seemed, did not end at death.

I carried that with me into the car on the drive to Lee, Massachusetts, two months later. The terror was real. The furniture flying around the house. The dark figure attacking Liz. All of it was real. But underneath the terror, something else was present too, a question that had been forming for years, growing sharper with every cold bedroom, every presence at the edge of vision, every impossible moment of confirmation like the one I had watched my grandmother deliver on that street in Ohio.

What is actually happening here?

The house in Lee was small and sandwiched between a dozen others on a side street, and a young couple, Daniel and Liz Scout, were sitting on the porch in the dark when we pulled up, waiting for us with the particular stillness of people who have run out of ordinary explanations.

As we entered the front door, the house was filled with the resounding pounding of massive invisible fists, slamming the walls in repetitions of three.

My grandfather calmly took it all in as though he had seen this a thousand times. "These repetitions of three are an indication we're dealing with something demonic."

My terror ratcheted up to an eleven. The sound was so loud I felt like I was vibrating.

At the time, I took my grandfather at his word. He was the expert. If he said three knocks meant demonic, then it must be true. It would be years before I started questioning whether we were actually dealing with demons or just putting a label on something we didn't fully understand. But that night, standing in that house with the walls shaking, I wasn't questioning anything. I was just trying not to run.

The first floor consisted of a small living room and kitchen, and a door that led to the tiny dark basement where they kept their washer and dryer. Many of the appliances and larger furniture had been removed because the family reported objects being thrown at them. Only a stove, refrigerator, sofa, and recliner remained downstairs.

As we climbed the stairs, the pounding continued and the walls shook. I could hear clawing and growling coming from inside them.

"Do you hear that growling?" I asked Paul. "Yeah," he replied nervously. At the top of the stairs, I peered into the bathroom on the left, and like something out of a Hollywood film, the large funeral-style crucifix on the wall was turned upside down.

There were three bedrooms upstairs, beds still in place but no dressers. The pull-down staircase to the attic that had previously knocked Liz senseless was pulled down.

My grandfather looked at me calmly. "Chris, I want you to sit in the dark in the master bedroom while we go downstairs and provoke this thing with holy church incense to make it reveal itself. Let us know if anything happens to you."

My first thought was: what exactly did he think was going to happen to me?

The use of religious provocation is an extraordinarily dangerous tactic, only to be used as a last resort in the most extreme circumstances. At the time I didn't understand that. I just trusted my grandfather to do what he felt was best.

"OK, Gramps," I said, and climbed up into the middle of the bed in the dark as they went downstairs, listening to the pounding and growling going on right behind my head and wondering when that huge hulking black figure would appear.

For the next hour I sat there, calling down to my grandfather in a squeaky voice.

"Gramps, I hear clawing and scratching in the wall right behind my head and there are growls coming out of the wall!"

"That's fine, Chris. Let us know if anything else happens."

What the hell was he expecting? I was sixteen years old, sitting in the dark in a room where something had already knocked a grown woman unconscious.

They smudged the entire downstairs, but every time they tried to bring the pot of holy church incense up the stairs it would go out. Once this type of incense gets going it is quite hard to extinguish. Something was putting it out deliberately.

After about an hour, everything died down and Paul came upstairs to relieve me. I went downstairs and listened to my grandfather interview the traumatized couple.

Around 10:00 PM we all sat in a circle trying to provoke the presence again. We received no response. We knew we were going on WTIC AM 1060 for an all-night radio program with host Brian Dow starting at midnight, a live call-in broadcast we would conduct over the phone. Liz and I took the opportunity to go to the local market for sandwiches before it started.

After we returned and had a late dinner, we got on the phones. Paul and Daniel were upstairs on one of the girls' princess phones. My grandfather and Liz were on the couch. I was in the recliner, phone in one hand, the large cross from the bathroom in the other.

As the program progressed, listeners called in and reported their rooms were getting deathly cold. That was also when we discovered the seven-second delay that is normally part of every radio program was inexplicably not working that evening.

My grandfather always taught me that 3 AM was the Devil's hour, and that night, as the clock struck the hour, all hell broke loose.

Two hulking black figures came down the stairs and stood on the landing, appearing to look at us. Even in a pitch-black room, these things were visible. Under my breath I commanded them to be gone in the name of Jesus Christ, as I had been taught.

At 3:15 Liz started screaming her face was on fire. My grandfather turned his flashlight on the left side of her face and, as we all watched, three claw marks raked down her cheek and blood dripped onto her chest.

Just then, the steel pot of holy church incense we had left in the kitchen came flying around the corner, straight at my head. At the last moment it veered away and slammed into the window behind me. The shade flew up with a terrifying crash. The heavy steel pot crumpled flat but the window did not break.

"Oh shit!" I yelled, live, over the radio, with no seven-second delay. Thousands of people heard it in real time.

Liz started begging to get out. I thought that was a terrific idea and ran for the front door as the lights began going on and off. I was standing right next to those two massive hulking entities, trying to get the door open, but though we had passed through it just hours earlier it would not move.

The recliner I had just been sitting in tumbled across the room toward me.

Then the door opened by itself and Liz and I ran out of the house, leaving my grandfather sitting calmly in the chaos, still reporting what was happening to the radio audience. I have never witnessed such courage in my life.

Once outside, one of us got physically ill. After all this time I cannot remember which of us it was.

Several months later, Father McKenna, a tiny, quiet, deeply holy man who had worked with my grandparents for years, came to bless the home. He moved through that house with the methodical calm of someone who had seen too much to be impressed by any of it, praying in Latin, marking doorways and windows with blessed salt and holy water, descending into the basement where black smoke had rolled up from no visible source. The pounding intensified. The smoke pressed outward as though aware of where it was being driven. And then, mid-strike, everything stopped. The smoke convulsed once and vanished. The house felt different. Lighter. As if something had been removed rather than simply frightened away.

He turned to the family and said, calmly, that it was not finished but had been pushed back. He gave them his instructions. He closed his ritual book. He left.

The case returned several months later. I was there for the second visit, when Liz showed us what appeared to be two claws that had pierced her scalp while she was doing laundry in the basement. I brought them to the University of Connecticut zoology department and was astounded by what came back: they were the two halves of the first premolar of a one- to two-year-old domesticated pig, broken in half. The roots looked like claws. They had been pushed into the poor woman's head.

Bishop McKenna returned, blessed the home and the family thoroughly, and the phenomena ended permanently.

My grandfather believed the family had been targeted because Liz had converted from Judaism. The pig's tooth seemed to him like confirmation. I questioned it even then. We were looking for explanations because none were obvious, and I was beginning to understand something about this work that would take years to articulate clearly: we are very good at naming things. We are considerably less good at understanding them. A name is not an explanation. It is the end of inquiry dressed up as the beginning of one.

That lesson has stayed with me for the rest of my life.

But it was not the lesson I took home from Lee that August night.

My grandfather had immersed me in the thing I feared most, and I had not been destroyed by it. I had run out the door. I had cursed on live radio. I had been afraid in a way that bypassed thought entirely and went straight to the body. And I had survived it. More than survived it. Something in me had shifted in that house, some internal weight had been quietly set down, and I didn't yet have language for what that meant.

I got home. I got into bed.

I reached over and turned off the light.

For the first time since I was eight years old, I lay in the dark and did not need to turn it back on.

The darkness was the same darkness it had always been. I was different. And somewhere in the distance between those two facts was everything I would spend the next forty years of my life trying to understand.

II. THE TRUTH UNDERNEATH

I have spent most of my life trying to understand the mind of God.

Sit with the arrogance of that sentence for a moment, because I did not see it as arrogance at the time. I saw it as inquiry. As the honest pursuit of truth through every available means. I was sixteen years old, the light was finally off, and I had questions I could not put down.

I moved through one religion and then another. I sat in catechism classes that raised more questions than they answered. I listened to the Mormons and the Jehovah's Witnesses, not to argue with them but to understand what they were actually pointing at beneath the doctrine. A Taoist handed me a book and something shifted. A professor of comparative philosophy named Dr. Grover sat with me for hours in his office, following ideas wherever they led without needing them to arrive anywhere in particular. I read the story of the Sioux shaman Black Elk. I sat with the Dalai Lama. I spent two years living and working with Animist communities in Mali during a military dictatorship. I spent time with the Kogi people of Colombia, one of the last intact pre-Columbian civilizations on earth, who speak of Aluna, the invisible thought-world they believe precedes and generates all of physical reality. I meditated in Buddhist temples in Thailand and Nepal. I engaged deeply with Hinduism's understanding of the Atman. I studied in Egypt and Israel. I worked within Umbanda traditions in

Brazil and Portugal. I engaged with witchcraft traditions in Veracruz, Mexico.

In each of these traditions, approached on its own terms, I found the same architecture underneath the different vocabularies. Awareness is primary. The physical world is its expression, not its source. The individual self is real but not ultimate.

That convergence is not coincidental. It only makes sense if what these traditions are perceiving is real, and what differs between them is the filter. The vocabulary. The hilltop they are standing on. Two people standing on opposite hilltops looking across the same valley are seeing the same landscape from different angles. Neither of them is wrong about what they see. But each of them is seeing only part of what is there.

It is only when they are willing to share what they see from where they stand that the whole picture begins to emerge. This is what beliefs do when we mistake them for facts. A belief shaped by genuine inquiry broadens what you can see. A belief shaped by fear narrows it. The first opens the hilltop to a wider view. The second builds walls around it and calls them truth. We go to war over our beliefs. We tear societies apart over them. We look for information that confirms what we already think and dismiss anything that does not fit, not because we are dishonest, but because this is what the mind does when the belief has become the lens rather than the conclusion. We stop looking at what is there and start looking for what we expect to find. What every tradition in this chapter has in common is that its founders looked first and concluded after. The Buddha sat under a tree and paid attention. Jesus went into the desert and paid attention.

The Kogi have been paying attention to Aluna for thousands of years. The moment any of their followers stopped paying attention and started defending the conclusion, the original perception began to calcify into doctrine. The hilltop became a fortress. This book is an attempt to climb down from the fortress and look at the valley.

But it was not only the spiritual traditions pointing in this direction.

I engaged seriously with quantum physics, consciousness studies, psychology, and cultural anthropology, not as a scientist, but as someone asking whether what I was observing across decades of real-life investigation was consistent with what researchers were finding at the edges of their own disciplines. What I found was that they were all arriving at the same address. Quantum entanglement demonstrates that particles once connected remain connected across any distance, instantaneously, in ways that defy ordinary assumptions about space and time. The block universe model in theoretical physics proposes that past, present, and future all exist simultaneously. And near-death experience research has documented perception during periods of confirmed flat brain activity. Each of these findings keeps arriving at the same address.

These are not spiritual claims. These are the findings of serious researchers working within rigorous methodologies. And they keep arriving at the same place that every genuine wisdom tradition has pointed toward for thousands of years.

Then I came across a projection from NASA.

The number of potentially living worlds in the observable universe, they estimated, exceeded the number of grains of sand on earth. I no longer remember the exact figure. What I remember is the number ceasing to be a number and becoming something else entirely. A weight. A silence. A reorientation of everything I thought I was doing.

I had been trying to understand the mind of whatever produced that. With this. A human brain. On one of those grains of sand.

The pride of it. The breathtaking, ignorant pride of it.

I realized that we are like three blind men touching different parts of an elephant, each one absolutely certain he understands what he is touching. One feels the trunk and knows it is a snake. One feels the leg and knows it is a tree. One feels the side and knows it is a wall. None of them is wrong about what they felt. All of them are wrong about what it is. And every one of them would argue passionately that the others are mistaken.

That image broke something open in me. Not my curiosity. Not my conviction that something real was there to be found. What broke was the certainty that I was capable of understanding it fully. That any of us are. Whatever sits at the center of all of this is so far beyond the reach of a human mind on a grain of sand in an unremarkable corner of one galaxy among billions that the attempt to contain it in any framework, scientific or spiritual or philosophical, is not inquiry. It is hubris.

And the moment I genuinely accepted that, the moment I stopped insisting on understanding and simply allowed myself to encounter what was there, I found what I had been looking for the entire time.

Not understanding. Faith.

I need to be precise about what I mean by that word, because it is one of the most abused words in the human vocabulary. I am not talking about blind faith. Blind faith asks nothing of you except that you stop asking questions. It outsources your judgment to an authority and calls the outsourcing virtue.

What I am describing is closer to a working hypothesis about your own life, one you test every day through the choices you make and the consequences that follow. I have noticed across decades that when my choices move toward helping others, toward genuine connection, the path opens. When they do not, it gets harder. I cannot prove that means anything. But I have seen it too consistently to dismiss.

My faith is this: that love is not a sentiment. It is the fundamental nature of what everything is when the illusion of separation falls away. And the clearest expression of that love, the most direct path toward whatever God actually is, is not prayer or doctrine or ritual. It is the moment when I reach into someone's darkness and help them find their way back to themselves. In that moment the illusion of separation between myself and another person dissolves completely, and what remains is the thing this entire book is trying to describe.

This is where the question of religion becomes unavoidable.

Every major spiritual tradition humanity has ever produced, when followed past the surface of its rituals and its institutional history, arrives at a version of this same recognition. In Hinduism, the Atman, the true self, is recognized as identical to Brahman, the universal consciousness underlying all existence. The individual is not separate from the whole. The individual is the whole, temporarily experiencing itself as separate. In Buddhism, the concept of Anatta, the absence of a permanent fixed self, points toward the same truth from a different direction. The Kogi speak of Aluna, the invisible thought-world that precedes and generates all physical reality. The ancient Egyptians understood the soul as having multiple aspects whose ultimate goal was the reunification of the individual expression with the eternal source.

In Kabbalah, the highest aspect of the soul is called Yechidah, the unified self connected directly to the divine. Christian mystics across centuries have spoken of the divine spark within each person. And Rumi described with overwhelming clarity the experience of the barrier between self and other finally dissolving.

These traditions emerged independently, across cultures that had no contact with each other, across millennia that shared no common language. And they keep describing the same thing.

Every one of these traditions was founded by human beings. And human beings are flawed. They carry the prejudices of their time and their culture. The men who wrote the scriptures encoded genuine perception of ultimate truth alongside tribal politics and cultural assumptions and justifications for things that had nothing to do with truth. And then institutions grew up around those texts, accumulated centuries of their own weight, and the original perception kept getting buried deeper under all of it.

This is why more people have been killed in the name of religion than for almost any other cause in human history. Not because the original teachers wanted that. Jesus of Nazareth did not want the Crusades. The Buddha did not want the ethnic nationalism being carried out in his name today. Every path has people on it who stopped climbing and mistook their resting place for the summit. Who follow the person standing in front of them rather than understanding where the path is actually leading.

The path is not the destination.

Religion can lead you to a spiritual connection. But a spiritual connection does not require religion. The mountaintop is real. Every genuine path is pointing toward it. What gets people lost is mistaking the path for the summit and spending the rest of their lives defending the road they chose instead of climbing.

And the story begins with a farmer, a horse, and an idea so simple it took me fifty years to fully understand it.

III. THE FARMER

There is an ancient Taoist parable, sometimes attributed to a farmer known as Sai Weng, whose precise origins are lost to history but whose wisdom has survived intact for thousands of years.

A farmer's horse runs away. His neighbors come to offer their condolences. What terrible luck, they say. The farmer looks at them and says: good, bad, who knows.

The next day the horse returns, and it brings with it a herd of wild horses. The neighbors come back. What wonderful luck, they say. The farmer says: good, bad, who knows.

His son tries to tame one of the wild horses. He is thrown and breaks his leg. The neighbors shake their heads. What terrible luck. The farmer says: good, bad, who knows.

The army comes through the village conscripting young men for a war. The son is passed over because of his broken leg. The neighbors say: what wonderful luck. The farmer says: good, bad, who knows.

The story has no ending. That is the point.

I did not encounter this parable until my early fifties. I was not ready for it before then. There is a saying that the teacher appears when the student is ready, and in my experience that has always proven true. The wisdom we need has a way of arriving precisely when we have been broken open enough to receive it. Not before. Not after. When the student is ready.

What the farmer understood is something most of us spend our entire lives resisting. That from inside a single lifetime, a single moment, a single perspective, we simply do not have enough information to know what anything ultimately means. The horse running away is not a catastrophe. It is a chapter. And we are not qualified to judge the book by any single chapter.

There is another story that has stayed with me. A monk is being walked to be beheaded. As he faces the executioner he notices one perfect strawberry on the ground. He reaches down, picks it, takes a bite, and a look of absolute bliss crosses his face. The executioner is astonished. Monk, he says, I am about to kill you. Why are you smiling? And the monk says: that is in the future. Right now I am enjoying a strawberry.

I used to think this story was about acceptance. About making peace with the inevitable. I understand it differently now. The monk is not resigned. He is fully present. The execution is real. The strawberry is also real. Both exist simultaneously. And the only moment in which he actually lives, the only moment available to any of us, is the one we are in right now. The storm is real. The brighter day on the other side of it is also real. The fact that you cannot see it from inside the storm does not mean it is not there.

We did not come here simply to be happy. That runs against almost everything our culture tells us about what life is for. We came here to learn. To grow. To be faced with obstacles that challenge us and opportunities to practice empathy and compassion and unconditional love. Happiness is not the destination. It is sometimes what arrives when we are fully engaged in the actual work of being here.

I know this not because I read it somewhere. I know it because I lived it.

When I was twenty-six years old, I was in Israel, building houses for the Israeli army with a Palestinian work crew during the first Intifada, or Palestinian uprising. I stepped backward through a hole in a roof and fell, herniating three discs in my back. It was the beginning of a long unraveling that I could not have predicted and would not have chosen. Over the years that followed the injuries worsened. I gained weight through inactivity. I lost mobility. I lost independence. I eventually lost the ability to work. I ended up in a wheelchair, on oxygen, requiring nursing care around the clock. My family wanted to put me in a rest home.

In between the fall and the wheelchair there were other losses. I lost a woman I loved deeply, my fiancée, to cancer. She died within two months of her diagnosis when her children and my son were still young. I lost the house we had built together. I lost the future we had imagined. I went into a depression that swallowed years. I became dependent on prescription opioids that left me barely functional. I lost my home. I lost nearly everything I owned. I was robbed by people I had welcomed in to care for me. I ended up homeless.

I am telling you this not for sympathy. I am telling you because when I talk about hitting rock bottom I am not speaking theoretically. I have been at the place where everything is gone and the people around you are suggesting that the rest of your life should be managed by strangers in a facility somewhere. That the story is essentially over. That what remains is just the waiting.

And even from that place, I kept showing up.

I continued to run the Warren Legacy Foundation from that wheelchair. Still talking to people in crisis. Still doing what I could to help others find their way through their own darkness even when I could not yet find my way through mine. I did not fully understand at the time why I kept doing that. Looking back I understand it completely. It was the thread that kept me connected to my own purpose when everything else had been stripped away. You cannot always help yourself out of the darkness directly. But you can show up for someone else. And in doing that something in you remembers what it is for.

What brought me out was not a single moment of personal heroism. It was a collective of people who chose to show up. Nurses who took the time to learn what could help me. People who believed I was worth the effort when I was not sure I believed it myself. I lost a hundred and forty-five pounds. I took my life back one decision at a time. And then something unexpected happened. Losing everything freed me.

I do not have the anchor of possessions and obligations and the accumulated weight of a conventional life holding me in place. I am out in the world now, moving through it, helping people across six continents, doing work that would not have been possible if I had held onto everything I lost. The fall through the roof in Israel was not a catastrophe. It was a chapter. The wheelchair was not the end of the story. Every loss was a thread being pulled into place in a picture I could not yet see.

I am not saying that suffering is secretly good. I am not saying that loss is a gift. I am saying that the story was not over when I thought it was. That what looked like the end was a door I had not yet learned to see.

What the farmer understood, and what I have come to understand through my own long education, is that there is a perspective larger than the one available from inside any single chapter of a life. A vantage point from which the broken leg and the returning horses and the army passing through are all visible at once. We do not have access to that perspective from where we stand. But we can learn to trust that it exists. To hold our judgments lightly enough that we do not close the door on what the next chapter might bring. To embrace change rather than fight it. Because change is not the enemy of the story. Change is how the story moves.

Whatever you are carrying right now, whatever loss or limitation or seemingly immovable obstacle has made you feel that the story is over, consider the possibility that you are the son with the broken leg and the army has not come through yet.

The chapter you are in is not the whole book. Good, bad, who knows.

But before you can fully trust that larger perspective, before it becomes something you feel rather than simply something you have read, you need to understand what you actually are. Not who. What. Because the answer to that question changes everything that follows.

IV. WHAT WE ACTUALLY ARE

Before anything else in this book can mean what I intend it to mean, we have to answer a question that most people never stop long enough to ask seriously.

What is a human being?

The conventional answer, the one embedded so deeply in modern Western culture that most people have never examined it, is that you are a biological organism. A body with a brain. And the brain, through processes that neuroscience is still working to fully map, produces the experience of being you. Your thoughts, your memories, your sense of self, your awareness of existing at all. All of it generated by approximately three pounds of tissue inside your skull. When the tissue stops functioning, you stop. The self that reads these words, that has loved and grieved and wondered and feared, simply ceases. Not transformed. Not continued. Ended.

That is not an unreasonable position. It is supported by a great deal of observable evidence. When you drink alcohol your personality changes. When you take certain medications, your mood shifts in ways that feel chemical rather than chosen. When someone you love experiences dementia you watch their personality dissolve piece by piece while their body continues. The correlation between brain state and the experience of selfhood is real and powerful and anyone who dismisses it without accounting for it is not thinking carefully enough.

That correlation is consistent with a different explanation than the one most people assume.

The brain does not generate consciousness. The brain receives it, tunes it, and expresses it through the particular instrument of a particular body in a particular lifetime. Consciousness exists independently of the brain. The brain is the means through which it operates in physical reality, not the source from which it springs.

Chris McKinnell as a child with his Irish setter Brandy. For twenty years after Brandy died, he continued to make his presence known. The first lesson about love that never ends.

Think of a radio. The radio does not generate the signal it plays. The signal exists independently, moving through the air, present whether or not any receiver is tuned to it. The radio receives that signal and translates it into something audible. A damaged radio does not disprove the signal. It distorts it. You get static. You get fragments. You get something recognizable but broken, something that tells you a transmission is there without being able to deliver it cleanly.

This is what traumatic brain injury actually demonstrates when you look at it carefully. A car with a damaged steering column handles completely differently than before the accident. That does not mean there is no driver. It means the driver is working with a compromised instrument. People who love someone who has experienced severe TBI consistently report the same thing. Beneath the changed behavior, beneath the personality the damage has altered, they recognize something of the original person. Something that persists. Something the damage has obscured but not eliminated. The radio is broken. The signal is still there.

My grandmother Lorraine Warren spent the final years of her life disappearing into Alzheimer's disease, as her mother and her brother had before her. It is a cruel illness precisely because of what it does to the receiver. Progressively, methodically, it damages the instrument through which a person expresses themselves in the world. She became nonverbal. She stopped recognizing people she had known and loved for decades.

Lorraine Warren with Chris McKinnell and a friend during the Great Britain investigation tour. Lorraine's capacity for genuine connection was evident in every room she entered.

I was with her on the last day of her life. After months of silence, after months of the disease having taken what seemed like everything, she looked at me with a smile on her face and told me she loved me.

The signal came through when it mattered most.

I was there. I watched the disease take her piece by piece for years. And in that final moment, with the instrument nearly gone, the consciousness that was Lorraine Warren found a way through anyway. The driver was still there. The car was barely running. And she used what remained to say what needed to be said.

This same dynamic plays out across the span of a single lifetime, not just in its final hours.

I am not the sixteen-year-old who walked into his first investigation with his grandfather, terrified and electrified in equal measure. I am not the young man who fell through a roof in Israel and began the long unraveling that would eventually put him in a wheelchair. I am not the man who sat in that wheelchair wondering if the story was already over. Each of those versions of me had a distinct personality, distinct fears, a distinct way of moving through the world. And yet something connects all of them across the decades. Something that has been present through every reinvention, every loss, every chapter that seemed like an ending and turned out to be a transition.

That something is not the personality. The personality changes constantly. It is contingent. It is responsive. It is real without being ultimate.

Your body is the car you drive.

While you are alive you are behind the wheel. The car and the driver are operating together, moving at the speed of physical life, engaged with the road, navigating traffic, responding to conditions. From the outside the driver and the vehicle appear to be one thing.

When you die the car breaks down. Not the driver. The car. The driver gets out and becomes a pedestrian. Still present. Still moving. But at a different speed, in a different space, no longer bound by the constraints that governed physical incarnated existence.

Consider what that road looks like at night.

It is dark. The drivers move through that darkness with their headlights, each pair illuminating a cone of road ahead. Most of the world beyond that cone is shadow. And in those shadows, at the edges of the road and beyond it, pedestrians move. They are there. They have always been there. But they are operating in a different space at a different pace and the darkness makes them nearly impossible to see.

This is why spirits appear most often in peripheral vision. Not because they are timid or incomplete. Because of the geometry of the encounter. You are moving at the speed of physical life. They are at the edge of your light. The peripheral vision is not a failure of perception. It is the accurate report of a real encounter at the limits of what the light can reach.

Not all headlights are equal. Some people move through the darkness with ordinary beams, illuminating the road directly ahead and little else. Others have exceptionally bright lights that push back the darkness further, revealing more of what lies alongside the road. What the first driver perceives as a terrifying shape in the darkness the second sees clearly enough to recognize as a person. As a consciousness. As something with somewhere to go and perhaps something to say.

This is what we call psychic sensitivity. It is not supernatural. It is not a gift bestowed on a chosen few. It is a matter of how much light you can bring to the darkness. The brighter the headlights the more clearly you can see what has always been there. And what has always been there is not a monster. It is a pedestrian. A person. Moving in the dark alongside the road, hoping someone will slow down long enough to see them.

This is also the foundation of what my grandfather and I called the law of recognition. When the living gather and speak of someone who has died, when they remember them, call their name, hold their image in mind, they are turning their headlights toward the dark. They are creating the conditions under which contact becomes possible. The remembering is the calling. The attention is the light.

You are not a body that happens to have consciousness. You are a consciousness that has, for now, a body.

The car my grandmother drove for ninety-two years finally broke down on a spring afternoon while I sat beside her. But in the last moment before it did, she looked at me with a smile I had known my entire life and told me she loved me.

The driver was still there. And when the time comes, the road will no longer be necessary.

If that is true, and I believe with everything I have that it is, then the experiences so many people have quietly carried, the presence felt in an empty room, the dream that was too real to be a dream, the moment of knowing something there was no ordinary way to know, are not signs that something is wrong with them. They are signs that they are picking up something genuine. And the question worth sitting with is not whether those signals exist. The question is what they are actually telling us.

V. THE WITNESS

I want to tell you what kind of witness I am before I tell you what I have witnessed.

I was fourteen years old the first time I witnessed something I could not explain. By the time I was sixteen I had seen enough that the question of whether consciousness survives death had stopped being philosophical for me. It had become personal. The question was no longer does this happen. The question was what does it mean that it does.

There is a difference between knowing something from inside your own experience and being able to demonstrate it to someone who has not had that experience. I have spent my life inside phenomena that most people encounter only as stories. That gives me a particular kind of knowing. It does not automatically give me proof.

What I can tell you is this. I have been a skeptic my entire professional life. Not the kind of skeptic who uses that word as a shield against anything that challenges a comfortable framework. The kind of skeptic who demands corroboration. Who asks what else could explain this before accepting any other explanation. Who has walked away from cases that turned out to have perfectly ordinary explanations without feeling that anything was lost. The discipline of this work is knowing the difference between what you saw and what you interpreted. Between what the evidence demonstrates and what it suggests.

My grandmother taught me that the best psychic in the world is right perhaps sixty percent of the time. That is an enormous margin of error to build decisions around, and I am not the best psychic in the world. It is a humbling standard and I apply it to myself first.

I learned that discipline partly from my grandmother Lorraine, who would not trust her own impressions without something to verify them against. I learned it partly from Dr. Kenneth Ring at the University of Connecticut, one of the world's leading researchers into near-death experiences, under whom I had the privilege of studying. Ring did not simply lecture. He brought in experiencers, ordinary people who had been through near-death experiences themselves, and had them speak directly to us. He had us keep daily journals of our own observations. Not impressions. Observations. Specific, dated, documented. The habit of writing down what actually occurred rather than what it felt like, of separating the experience from the interpretation, shaped everything I have done in the field since.

What he gave me was not a belief system. It was a methodology. And it is the methodology I bring to everything that follows.

Let me give you an example. In 2021 I was working in Costa Rica. A team of investigators had flown in from Mexico to work with me. They brought me to the ruins of a home overlooking the capital, San Jose, the city lights twinkling beautifully far below us. I had no idea why we were there, nor did I ask for details. They asked me to tell them what I sensed. As I made my way down the crumbling stairs alongside what must have been a beautiful home at one time I could feel my neck tightening, and I had trouble swallowing. As I reached the terrace underneath the house, it was one place in particular where I felt like I was strangling. One of the researchers confirmed that the man who had lived there had hung himself in that exact location.

I asked "was he a gringo?" meaning a man from the United States.

'Yes" came the solemn reply from Alma Rayas, leader of the team, "Was he ex-United States military?" I asked.

Again, Alma nodded.

That independent verification of what I was sensing was necessary for me to feel comfortable to continue. But it is important to understand that what happened next was subjective.

I felt the spirit telling me that he was happy and didn't want to leave, but I felt that wasn't true. He was terrified. Another medium from Alma's team named Caroline was with me. While the rest of the team used their instruments to take readings, we walked away and tried to communicate with the spirit. He seemed far more at ease with Caroline.

Through 30 minutes of counseling we were able to understand that he had killed his two dogs before killing himself because he didn't want them to suffer. When he died and realized he was still consciously aware, he became terrified of passing over because he thought he would go to hell.

The videographer that had brought us to this location confirmed also that the dogs had been killed.

We were finally able to help him to pass over without fear. I have learned that hell is something we impose on ourselves. It is separation from whatever we wish to think of as God, hiding in the darkness far from its light.

On another occasion in 2025, I was called to a home in Asuncion Paraguay. The woman had sent me video showing her bedroom door, shaking and opening by itself. She was afraid she was dealing with demons, which is not an uncommon belief when people are facing something that terrifies them. I agreed to go the next day.

That night, at 2 AM, there were three loud raps on my bedroom door. It is not uncommon for the spirits to try to intimidate me before I enter a home for the first tie, but I didn't feel anything negative with this visitation.

I said firmly, but respectfully, "I'm coming to your house tomorrow. You do not have my permission to bother me at home. I will be there soon. You must leave now."

The spirit immediately slipped away.

The next day I sat with the family, and I could feel that it was her father who had just died. At first, I thought he simply wanted her to know that she was not alone because she felt very isolated. After I left, the phenomena continued, and I agreed to go back to do a spiritual cleansing if it was necessary.

When I arrived with my daughter, I asked if I could sit upstairs in the master bedroom by myself where most of the activity was taking place to see if I could communicate with the spirit. As I sat on the woman's bed, I kept hearing the word danger, danger, danger. I told the spirit that I wasn't going to tell this family that they were in danger without giving them some concrete reason to believe that.

As I prepared to do the spiritual cleansing of the home, I noticed that there were liquor bottles and beer bottles all over the kitchen and storage area. I asked about this and suggested that it was a bad idea if they were dealing with a haunting.

The woman said "that doesn't belong to me and my son. That was my ex-boyfriend."

I immediately knew where the danger was coming from. "Is your ex-boyfriend dangerous?"

"Yes. Terribly. He has threatened us and beaten my son. He left us and he's already with another woman, but he still demands money from me," she said timidly.

I am not a gun enthusiast and my first impulse is never to consider violence, but I immediately asked her "do you have a gun?"

"Yes but it's at my mother's house," she said. "I think you better get it just to be safe."

That night she told a WhatsApp group that she was in that I had been to her home and the man found out. He threatened to kill me and her mother, if the woman did not give him more money.

Sometimes the danger isn't the shaking bedroom door. It's the living person that you were sharing the bed with.

I'm happy to report that they were able to move and that they are safe today. I still check on them occasionally.

Not every case involves a threat from the living. Some of the most significant moments in this work have come quietly, in the dark, with no instruments running and no team present.

This pattern of specific details confirmed by independent sources, or of witnesses who have no reason to expect what they encounter, has been the standard I hold myself to. Not what I feel alone. What can be verified. Not the intensity of the experience. The accuracy of the detail.

Some experiences have broken my heart, but I will be grateful for them forever.

Her name was Dyanna. She was someone I loved and who loved me and whose death left things between us unfinished in ways neither of us had chosen. She was my fiancee, diagnosed with cancer and dead within two months of her diagnosis. In her final weeks she had been pulling away from me the way people sometimes do when they are dying, gathering themselves inward, letting go of the things of this life. It left things unsaid between us that needed to be said.

The night she died I was sitting at my desk writing her a letter. I did not know she was dying as I wrote. The letter said that cancer was not going to kill our love. That I wanted to come see her. That I loved her. I was reaching toward her in the very moment she was leaving.

Her mother and sister came to my door the next morning to tell me she was gone. I collapsed.

Chris McKinnell with Dyanna. She died within two months of her cancer diagnosis, leaving things between them unfinished in ways neither had chosen. She came back to finish them.

The night before her funeral I was lying in the dark when Dyanna came to me. She kept saying it's okay. It's okay. Everything is fine now. I was crying, not gently, the kind that comes from somewhere below language. And fine was not enough. Fine was not the thing that was unfinished between us. The love itself was unfinished. The words were unfinished. And I think she knew it too because two weeks later she came back.

I woke in the pitch black of that bedroom. I heard footsteps coming down the hallway. She was a heavier woman and I knew her footsteps. There was no question in my mind whose they were. When I opened my eyes there was a mirror on the back of the bedroom door. I should not have been able to see anything in that darkness. I could see her in the mirror behind me in the bed, propped on one elbow, looking down at me with a smile I knew.

I closed my eyes immediately. I did not want to see her leave again. That is not logical and I know it. But I could not live with watching her go a second time.

She moved in front of me. I heard her voice, audible in the room, not inside my head, say "I. Love. You." One word at a time. Clearly and slowly. Then she kissed me on the lips. I felt her lips on mine, with pressure and warmth. And then she was gone.

She had needed me to know how she really felt. Not how the illness and the necessary distance and the pulling away had made things appear at the end. She came back to finish what had been left unfinished. And when it was finished, she left.

I am telling you this as a witness. I was awake. I heard her before I saw her. I felt the kiss. These are specific sensory details from a specific moment. I have spent my professional life learning to distinguish genuine contact from grief-driven hallucination and this was neither of those things.

What Dyanna's return showed me, and what I have seen confirmed across thousands of cases since, is that the unresolved pull of love and unfinished business does not dissolve at the moment of death. It persists. It draws consciousness back toward what it could not release. This is not a romantic idea. It is one of the most consistent observations in my body of work, and it carries a shadow as well as a light.

My grandmother Lorraine has visited me many times since her death. I want to tell you about two occasions that were independently witnessed.

The first was during a Christmas gathering on a video call with members of the foundation. I was sharing stories about my grandparents and the way they had celebrated the holidays with people they loved. Suddenly the hair on my right arm stood up. The woman to my left looked at me and smiled and said your grandmother just said Christopher, we're here. I had already registered something in that moment, before she spoke. The perception arrived in both of us at the same time, confirmed by her before I acknowledged anything.

The second was during an interview in Lima, Peru. The interviewer asked me whether my grandparents were with me. I said no, and I believed it. At that moment I felt myself get hugged. A specific physical sensation, unmistakable. The medium sitting next to me had a look of pure shock on her face. She had perceived something before I gave any verbal acknowledgment. I said wait a minute. Yes. They are, and laughed.

In both cases the confirmation came from an independent witness before I said anything. That is the standard I hold everything to.

Sanatorio Duran sits above the clouds. That is not a figure of speech. The complex is built into the mountainside above San Jose at an elevation where the clouds gather below the ridgeline, and on clear days the peaks around it look like islands floating on a white sea. It is one of the most visually stunning places I have ever stood. It is also one of the most saturated with residual pain I have ever entered.

I knew almost nothing about the place when I arrived. I knew it was a former sanatorium. I knew it was now a tourist attraction of sorts. That was the extent of it. A team had brought me there. Reporters were following us that day, which I found uncomfortable. The work I do does not perform well for cameras, and whatever was in that building did not deserve to be made into spectacle.

We entered the children's ward. In one of the bathrooms I stopped. I felt clearly that a child had taken their own life there, hanging from a support beam. The feeling was specific and overwhelming and I could not move past it. One of the reporters who was with us witnessed my reaction in that room. What I had felt was later confirmed. A child had died there, in that manner, close to a century earlier.

As we moved through the complex I became aware of a building higher up the hill, above the main sanatorium. I had not been told anything about it. But I felt immediately that the man who had lived there was the one in charge of the facility, and that he had known everything that was happening to the children inside it, and had hidden it to protect his own reputation. That too was confirmed. The building had been the residence of the doctor who ran the facility. The cover-up of the abuse that had taken place under his watch was documented. I had felt what I felt before anyone told me what it was. That is the only way I know how to work.

I managed to slip away from the group and find a room alone. A child appeared to me. I could not tell if it was a boy or a girl. Small. Still. Looking at me with the particular wariness of something that has been alone for a very long time and does not know whether to trust what it sees. I spoke in my broken Spanish, trying to explain that this was not where they belonged anymore, that their parents were waiting on the other side, that all they had to do was call out and their parents would come. The child would not move. The fear was too deep. I was not getting through.

Then I became aware of my grandfather standing to my right. Ed Warren, arms folded, watching me. That expression I knew from years of working alongside him, somewhere between patience and mild exasperation. As if to say, Chris. What exactly are you doing. And my grandmother came through the doorway. She walked to the child, got down on one knee, and held out her hand. The child took it without a word. They went into the light together.

Chris McKinnell with his grandfather Ed Warren and fellow investigator Ray Jefferson during a three-thousand-mile tour of the most haunted locations in Great Britain. Ray Jefferson, a dear friend and extraordinary colleague, has since passed. The tour they built together is one Chris is recreating for a new generation.

I cannot offer what happened in that room under the same evidentiary standard as what came before it. I was alone. There was no witness. What I can tell you is that I have spent over forty years learning to distinguish what I genuinely perceive from what fear or imagination produces, and that what I experienced in that room did not feel like either of those things. Visitations from my grandparents had been corroborated in the past, and I had no reason to doubt this experience.

The quality of the air in that room changed when they were gone. Something that had been fixed in that place for nearly a century was no longer there. My grandparents are still working. I find that I am not surprised by this, and I do not worry about them.

I came back down from the mountain that evening carrying all of it. That night something woke me at two in the morning. Given what I had walked through that day, I assumed the worst. I was wrong about that, but I did not find out until the following afternoon. That story belongs a few pages from now. What matters here is that I came down from that mountain having felt things that were confirmed and having witnessed something that was not. I know the difference. I am telling you both.

There is one more account I want to share, and it is one I have sat with for a long time before feeling ready to put it on the page. Not because I doubt it. Because of what it means.

About a year and a half ago, roughly six months before the museum and the house were sold, my grandmother came to me in a dream. I want to be precise about what I mean by that, because there is a difference between an ordinary dream and a visitation that most people who have experienced both will recognize immediately. An ordinary dream dissolves the moment you open your eyes. A visitation stays with you. The quality of it is different, more real than waking life in a way that is impossible to describe to someone who has not felt it. This was a visitation.

I was in her house. I had brought friends with me and I was taking them downstairs to show them the museum, the room filled with the artifacts of decades of investigation that had been part of my life since childhood. I opened the door to the corridor that leads out to it.

The corridor was empty. The museum was gone. Everything was gone.

I stood there in shock for a moment, not understanding what I was seeing. Then I turned around.

My grandmother was sitting across the room. Exactly as I had always known her. Smiling at me with the smile I had known my entire life.

"Gram," I said. "What happened? Everything's gone."

She smiled and said, "Don't worry about that, honey. How's your project coming along? How's the book coming along?"

And then it dawned on me.

"Gram," I said. "You're dead."

She just smiled. "Don't worry, honey. How is the book coming along? You have to finish it."

I understood in that moment that I was in the presence of something real. Not a dream. Her. And I felt exactly what you would expect to feel in the presence of someone you love who you have not seen in years. Joy. Relief. The specific quality of being known completely by someone who loves you without condition.

"I promise, Gram," I told her. "I will get it done. I'm trying. It hasn't been easy. I have so many thoughts, so much research. But you have my word."

I woke up then, her sweet smile still in my mind's eye.

I understood that exchange fully only in retrospect, after the house and the museum were sold. She had shown me an empty corridor before it happened. Whether that was her way of preparing me or simply evidence that she was already aware of what was coming, I can't say for sure. What I can say is that the book she asked me to finish is the one you are holding now. And that she apparently wanted to make sure I had everything I needed to help people want to read it.

Which brings me to Sandy.

Around the year 2000, a woman named Sandy, a friend of my grandmother's from years earlier, had called her about paranormal activity she was experiencing at home. My grandmother, wanting to help, thought of a project my grandfather had been quietly working on. He had been recording what he called angelic music directly into a cassette, along with spoken prayers and careful instructions for how to use it properly. My grandmother believed he had made multiple copies and sent one to Sandy, thinking it might bring her some peace and protection.

It was the only copy in existence.

Sandy kept it for twenty-five years. She treasured it as a memento of two people she had loved and respected, not fully understanding what she was holding.

In 2025 Sandy traveled to New Orleans, where Annabelle was on tour. She went to meet with Lorraine's family. What she found instead troubled her. The crowds were pressed up against the Annabelle box, being urged to touch it. She did not see any family present. She asked about me specifically, because my grandmother had always talked about me, about how much she loved me, about what she hoped I would do with the legacy they had built together. Sandy had been looking for me.

Although the people running the tour tried to take it, she decided the cassette needed to go to me.

The night before she sent the package, her adult son got up in the night to use the bathroom. He was in his underwear and became very embarrassed when he saw an older woman with a hair bun standing in the doorway of his parents' bedroom. She was holding a chicken. She looked at him and smiled. Then she was gone.

Lorraine Warren holding one of her beloved chickens, exactly as Sandy's son described seeing her the night before the package arrived, in a dream visitation that led to the recovery of Ed Warren's final recorded workshop. Sandy had kept the recording for twenty-five years, waiting without knowing why.

He told his mother the next morning. He had no idea who the woman was. He had never heard of Lorraine Warren. What he could not have known was that my grandmother loved her chickens so much that they lived inside the house with her. It was one of those details known only to people who had actually been close to her personally.

He simply described what he saw. And what he described was specific, personal, and accurate in a way that had no ordinary explanation.

The package arrived. Inside the box was a padded envelope. The handwriting on it was my grandmother's. I recognized it immediately because she had sent me greeting cards for every conceivable holiday for as long as I could remember, and I had kept them all. That handwriting had been part of my life for decades. Seeing it on a package that had traveled to me through a woman my grandmother had apparently visited the night before it was sent, carrying the only recording of my grandfather's final work that exists in the world, is not something I have words adequate to describe.

Readers of the special edition of this book will be able to hear that recording. My grandfather's voice. The prayers. The angelic music he believed had been given to him. The work he did quietly, alone, that my grandmother made sure found its way home. She asked me to finish the book. I promised her I would.

Thank you, Gram. It's finished.

I have shared these accounts not to convince you of anything but to show you the pattern. In every one of them the significant detail arrived before the explanation. The identification came after the description. The witness had no framework for what they encountered and no reason to invent the specific thing they reported.

The dead, it seems, are not finished with us the moment we assume they are. And the love that connects us does not require a heartbeat to remain real.

Which raises a question I spent years trying to push away, because the answer kept arriving from directions I had not expected and could not dismiss. If love persists after death, what exactly is doing the persisting? The answer to that question is not mystical. It has been documented in peer-reviewed journals, measured in clinical settings, and arrived at independently by researchers who started from the opposite end of the argument from where I did. And it changes everything.

VI. THE EVIDENCE

There is a remarkable experiment worth starting with because it cuts directly to the heart of something every investigator eventually has to reckon with.

Researchers shaped a log to roughly resemble the Loch Ness monster and placed it in the water at Loch Ness. Between ten and twenty percent of the people who saw it had an immediate visceral reaction that it was the monster. Upon closer examination they knew better. But the first response was the creature. When the identical log was placed in a nearby loch with no legendary association, not a single person saw a monster. They saw a log. The stimulus was identical. The cultural framework was different. And the cultural framework determined what people perceived before their rational mind had a chance to examine what was actually there.

This is not a story about gullible tourists. This is a story about how human perception works. The mind reaches for the nearest available explanation when confronted with the unfamiliar. It reaches into the cultural vocabulary it has been given, finds the closest match, and presents that match as perception before the conscious mind has had a chance to weigh in. By the time you are examining the experience the label is already attached.

A lifetime of facing the extraordinary in this field taught me that the willingness to say I don't know is not a defeat. It is the only starting point that leads anywhere worth going. The moment I stopped needing to name what I was encountering and started simply following what the evidence actually showed, everything changed. The phenomena became more interesting, not less. The questions became more precise. And the answers, when they came, were considerably more reliable than anything the old framework had been providing.

With that in mind, I want to walk you through two ideas from physics that will keep appearing throughout this book, because they deserve to be understood clearly rather than simply referenced as impressive-sounding concepts.

The first is the block universe. Most of us experience time as a river, carrying us forward from the past into the future. But Einstein's theory of relativity calls this into question. According to the mathematics of relativity, past, present, and future do not flow. They exist simultaneously. Time is not a river. It is a landscape. Every moment that has ever happened and every moment that will ever happen exists right now, the way every page of a book exists simultaneously even though you can only read one page at a time. From inside time we experience sequence. From outside time there is only the whole. This is not a fringe idea. It is the logical consequence of the most rigorously tested theory in the history of physics. And its implications are extraordinary. If all moments exist simultaneously, the past is not gone. It is next door.

The second is the holographic universe. A hologram is a two-dimensional surface that encodes a three-dimensional image. What makes it remarkable is that every part of the hologram contains the whole image. If you cut a hologram in half, each half does not show half the picture. Each half shows the entire picture at lower resolution. The part contains the whole. Physicist David Bohm proposed that the universe itself may work this way, that what we experience as separate distinct physical reality is the surface expression of a deeper undivided wholeness in which everything is enfolded into everything else.

The mystics of a dozen traditions had been saying the same thing for centuries. Bohm arrived there through equations. They were describing the same thing.

Hold both of those ideas close. They are going to keep coming up.

In 2001 a cardiologist named Pim van Lommel published the results of a prospective study in The Lancet, one of the most prestigious medical journals in the world. He and his colleagues had followed 344 patients in ten Dutch hospitals who had been successfully resuscitated after cardiac arrest. What made this study different from everything that had come before was the methodology. Van Lommel's team documented each patient's account immediately after resuscitation, before memory could fade or be shaped by suggestion. They verified that every patient had been clinically dead with a flat EEG during the period of their reported experiences. They ruled out oxygen deprivation, medication effects, and prior familiarity with near-death experience accounts.

What they found was that a meaningful percentage of patients reported accurate and specific perceptions of events occurring in the physical environment during the period when their brains showed no measurable activity whatsoever. One patient accurately described the nurse who had removed his dentures and the specific drawer she had placed them in. He had been unconscious with his eyes closed the entire time. He had no ordinary means of knowing any of this. He described it correctly.

Van Lommel's conclusion was that current scientific understanding cannot account for these experiences and that consciousness may have aspects that function independently of brain activity. A cardiologist. Publishing in The Lancet. That is not a fringe claim. That is a peer-reviewed conclusion from one of medicine's most important journals.

Pam Reynolds followed the evidence even further. In 1991 she underwent a surgery so dangerous it required her body temperature to be lowered to sixty degrees, her heart stopped completely, and all blood drained from her brain. Her EEG was flat. A device inserted in her ear before the surgery began prevented an auditory information from reaching her.

Her eyes were taped shut. By every clinical standard she was not conscious and was not capable of consciousness.

Under those conditions she watched her own surgery from above the operating table.

She described the specific bone saw used to open her skull, an instrument she had never seen and had no way of knowing existed. She accurately described a conversation between two members of the surgical team about the condition of her femoral artery. Both descriptions were verified by the surgical team. Every sensory channel had been deliberately blocked. What she reported should not have been possible. It happened anyway.

Then there is the case that I find most compelling of all, precisely because of who it happened to.

Eben Alexander spent his career as a Harvard-trained neurosurgeon explaining away near-death experiences. He had the vocabulary to dismiss every account he encountered with scientific confidence. In 2008 he contracted a rare form of bacterial meningitis that shut down his neocortex completely for seven days. The part of the brain he had spent his career identifying as the generator of conscious experience was not functioning. He reports a detailed and coherent encounter with consciousness outside the physical, including a meeting with a figure he did not recognize. After his recovery his family showed him a photograph of a biological sister he had not known existed. She had died years earlier. The figure he had encountered was her.

Some neurologists have argued that the experience may have occurred during the transition into or out of the coma rather than during the period of flat brain activity. These are legitimate objections and they deserve to be heard. But they address the timeline, not the experience itself. They do not explain how a man who did not know he had a biological sister encountered a figure who turned out to be exactly that.

The next researcher and her groundbreaking study makes us question the very nature of time. Julia Mossbridge and her colleagues conducted a meta-analysis of studies examining whether people exhibit measurable physiological responses to stimuli before those stimuli are presented. Not after. Before. The body responding to something that has not yet happened. The results were consistent, the methodology was rigorous, and the findings have been replicated across independent laboratories. If the body can respond to a future event before that event occurs, then the model of time we all take for granted is not consistent with how awareness actually operates. In a block universe, where all moments exist simultaneously, information from the future is not impossible. It is simply information from a part of the landscape the conscious mind has not yet reached. The body, it seems, sometimes gets there first.

The University of Virginia's Division of Perceptual Studies has been documenting cases of children who remember previous lives for over fifty years. The work was begun by Ian Stevenson and continued by Jim Tucker. Researchers interview the child and document their specific statements before any attempt is made to verify them. They then investigate independently to determine whether the statements match the life of a deceased individual the child could not have known about. The cases that meet their evidentiary standard number in the thousands.

James Leininger is one of the most thoroughly documented. Born in 1998 in Louisiana, by the age of two he was having nightmares about a plane crash and demonstrating knowledge of World War II aircraft that no two-year-old could have acquired from his environment. He named the aircraft carrier his plane had taken off from. He named a fellow pilot. He described being shot down over a specific location in the Pacific. Every verifiable detail held. The ship existed. The pilot he named was real and had died in combat.

Japanese records confirmed the specific engagement he described. American veterans who had served on that ship met the family and confirmed details James knew that were not in any public record.

There is more than one explanation consistent with this evidence, and intellectual honesty requires acknowledging that. The first is a specific unresolved consciousness returning to work through what it could not release, karma as gravitational pull, the ego's refusal to let go drawing it back into incarnation. The second is that if consciousness is ultimately one, if the holographic principle is real and every part contains the whole, then what James Leininger may have accessed is not his own previous life but the accumulated experience of the whole, a record that every experience which has ever occurred remains encoded in the fabric of reality itself. In a holographic universe, a young child whose neurological filters have not yet been fully built might tap into that record with a clarity that most adults have long since filtered out.

The evidence does not settle which explanation is correct. Both are consistent with everything else in this book, and I hold both with equal seriousness.

The evidence in this chapter does not prove that consciousness survives death. What it does is something more important than proof. It shows you that the experiences you may have quietly carried, the sense of a presence you could not explain, the dream that felt too real to be a dream, the moment of knowing something you had no ordinary way of knowing, are not signs that something is wrong with you. They are signs that you are human. That you are picking up signals that have always been there. That the universe is considerably more alive and more connected than the framework most of us were handed at birth has room to hold.

You are not imagining things. You are perceiving things that your culture may not have given you language to describe. And the question of why some people develop that language and others never do, why some traditions cultivate these capacities across generations while others have spent centuries trying to stamp them out entirely, is the question that leads us into the most uncomfortable territory of all.

VII. THE CITY OF THE DEAD

In 1991 I walked into a cemetery where people were raising their children among the tombs, cooking their meals between the crypts, and living by a set of rules about what shared the space with them that had been refined over centuries of direct experience.

Nobody there had ever heard of Ed and Lorraine Warren. They didn't need to.

It was January. I was twenty-six years old, two months out of Israel, and I did not yet know what I had done to myself.

The fall through the roof had happened in late November. The first weeks were bad enough that I knew something was seriously wrong, but the human body has a remarkable capacity for denial when it is young and the world is still offering itself to you. I had spent Christmas in the Sinai desert, in a village called Dahab on the Red Sea, and then made my way to Cairo. The pain was there. I managed it. I had no idea I was walking around on injuries that would compound over the next 17 years into a wheelchair and a life I could not have imagined from where I stood then, moving freely through one of the oldest cities on earth.

Near the youth hostel where I was staying there was a small pizza place, and the two young men cooking there became my companions for those weeks in Cairo. They were funny and generous and curious about everything, and when they learned what I did and why I had come to Egypt, they offered to take me somewhere most tourists never went.

They brought me to Al-Qarafa. The City of the Dead.

Al-Qarafa has been a burial ground since the Islamic conquest of Egypt in the seventh century. It is vast, stretching for miles along the edge of Cairo, a city of tombs and crypts and mausoleums that in another context might seem simply historical. But Cairo is a city of profound economic disparity, and since the end of the Second World War, some of its most destitute residents have been living among the dead. They have run electricity and water into their makeshift homes between the graves. They have raised children there. They have built a community inside a cemetery, and that community has its own rules, its own understanding of what shares the space with them, and its own long experience of what happens when those rules are ignored.

What they live alongside are the djinn.

In the West, the word calls up pantomime figures from children's stories, genies in bottles granting wishes. That image has almost nothing to do with what the djinn actually are within Islamic tradition, or with what the people of Al-Qarafa understand themselves to be living among. The djinn appear in Arabic literature as far back as the sixth century BCE and were incorporated into Islamic belief in the seventh century CE. They are described as beings created from smokeless fire before the creation of humanity, possessed of free will, capable of being benevolent, destructive, or entirely indifferent to human concerns. The most powerful and malevolent among them, Iblis, refused to bow before Adam and was cast from heaven. He is the Islamic understanding of what the West calls Satan. But the djinn are not a single category of being any more than humanity is. They are a population. And like any population, they contain multitudes.

In Al-Qarafa, many djinn have been called upon across centuries to protect specific tombs or to curse those who trespass. The residents know which places to avoid. They do not avoid them out of superstition. They avoid them the way you avoid a downed power line, because the consequences of not doing so have been demonstrated, repeatedly, across generations of people who live close enough to the evidence to take it seriously.

One of my companions that day had grown up in the cemetery. He knew its geography the way a person knows their own neighborhood, which streets are safe, which corners to cross carefully, which doors not to open. His older brother had died fighting against Israel years before. He told me this without bitterness, blaming the governments rather than the people, and said that Israelis visited Egypt all the time and were always welcome. He wished only that people on both sides could live in peace. I had just come from Israel. I had been building houses there with a Palestinian work crew when I fell. He did not know any of that. He simply invited me into his world.

Because of his presence, and because I was with him, the inhabitants of Al-Qarafa were willing to speak with me. They showed me several abandoned tombs, places that others had tried to occupy and from which they had been driven out, or worse.

I walked through spaces that afternoon where the air itself felt different. Not dramatically. Not the way it does in films, with sudden temperature drops and lights flickering on cue. More the way a room feels when something significant happened in it and the walls have not yet forgotten. There were places I had to step back from, not because I saw anything, but because whatever was present did not want to be examined and made that clear in a way that bypassed thought entirely and went straight to the body. I protected myself and kept moving.

One of the phenomena associated with a particular category of djinn, called ghuls, is the abduction of humans who wander where they should not. Many people go missing in Al-Qarafa. Whether a non-human predator accounts for any of those disappearances is a question I cannot answer. What I can tell you is that an older woman I sat with that afternoon told me a story that has never left me.

She had two children. One of them, a little girl of about five, had climbed up onto a tomb, the way five-year-olds do everywhere in the world, careless and delighted with themselves. But this was a tomb that the adults of the community knew to be protected, one of the places with a history that made the rules around it absolute. The woman saw her daughter up there and screamed for her to get down. The child was startled and fell off the far side of the grave.

She was never seen again.

The woman and her neighbors searched everywhere. There was no sign that the child had hit the ground when she fell. No injury. No trace. The grave was not high. There was nowhere for a five-year-old to go. And yet she was gone.

I did not try to explain what she had told me. I had spent years by then learning to distinguish between the impulse to name something and the discipline of staying with what the evidence actually showed. And what the evidence showed, in that cemetery on that afternoon, was a community of people with centuries of accumulated experience living alongside phenomena that the frameworks I had grown up with could not adequately contain. They were not frightened in the way a Western family becomes frightened when something moves in their house. They were not reaching for exorcists or cameras or explanations. They had simply incorporated what was there into the way they lived, the way people incorporate any reality that cannot be changed. Certain tombs you do not climb on. Certain places you do not enter after dark. Certain presences you acknowledge and leave alone.

It was the most sophisticated relationship with the paranormal I had ever witnessed, and it was being practiced by people who had never heard of Ed and Lorraine Warren and had no use for any vocabulary I had brought with me from Connecticut.

Whatever label you apply to what took that child does not change what happened to her. The label is not the reality. I had understood that intellectually for years. Standing in that cemetery, I felt it for the first time.

Twenty-three years later, in 2014, the djinn reached me again. I was in my wheelchair by then, the injuries from that Israeli roof having finally compounded into the full weight of what they always were. A man in Cairo contacted me for help. Someone beneath him at work, wanting his position, had obtained a cursed object and arranged for it to be placed in his possession. It was a doll. He believed a djinn had been bound to it with deliberate harmful intent, and the phenomena in his home, the activity around his young daughter, had convinced him he was right.

He was going to send it to me. He packed it into the trunk of his car and drove toward the post office.

He called me on the way. I was thousands of miles from Cairo, in a wheelchair, and a man was on the phone telling me that his car was being struck from behind by something that was not there. Again and again, as he drove. The impacts were real. The car was being hit. There was nothing behind him.

The doll never reached the post office. He turned back.

I worked with him remotely over the following weeks, guiding him through what needed to be done, drawing on every tradition I had ever worked within to find the approach that fit his cultural and spiritual context. Not my framework. His. What mattered was not the vocabulary. It was the genuine focused intention behind it. The doll was eventually dealt with. The activity stopped. His daughter was not harmed.

I thought about that afternoon in Al-Qarafa the entire time. About the people who had built their lives around a knowledge that most of the world dismissed as primitive superstition. About the woman whose daughter fell behind a tomb. About what it means that the same force, or something indistinguishable from it, could reach from a car in Cairo to a wheelchair in another country twenty-three years later as though distance were simply not a relevant consideration.

Quantum entanglement demonstrates that particles once connected remain connected regardless of the distance separating them. The block universe model holds that all moments exist simultaneously, that what we experience as separation in space and time is a feature of perception rather than of reality. The researchers whose work filled the previous chapter arrived at those conclusions through mathematics and clinical methodology and peer-reviewed publication.

The people of Al-Qarafa arrived at the same place through centuries of living inside the evidence.

Neither group was wrong about what they were describing. They were simply standing at different points on the same perimeter, looking inward at the same thing.

That night, after a home-cooked meal at his family's home, one of the young men who had brought me to the City of the Dead took the ring from his finger and handed it to me. It had been a gift from his girlfriend. He wanted me to have it. He told me that when I returned to Egypt I would always have a home with his family.

I have not been back to Egypt. But I still have the ring. It is in a small box at my mother's house, among the handful of things I managed to save when I lost everything else. The treasures. The ones that mattered most.

His brother died fighting against the country I had just come from. He fed me in his home and gave me something irreplaceable and asked for nothing.

There is no framework that contains that either. But it points at the same place everything else points.

The people of Al-Qarafa did not need a framework. They had something older and more reliable. They had practice.

VIII. HOW WE ACCESS WHAT LIES BEYOND

Every culture that has ever existed on this earth, without exception, has developed practices specifically designed to quiet the noise of ordinary existence long enough to perceive something beyond it. Meditation. Fasting. Drumming. Vision quests. Sweat lodges. Plant medicine journeys. Sensory deprivation. Rhythmic chanting. Deep contemplative prayer. The specific forms differ enormously. The underlying structure is identical. Quiet the instrument sufficiently, in enough different ways, across enough different centuries and continents, and something consistent comes through.

This is not coincidence. And it is not adequately explained by the fact that all human brains share the same basic architecture. That explanation accounts for the mechanism of access. It does not account for what is being accessed. A radio tuned to the same frequency in different countries receives the same signal not because all radios are built similarly but because the signal is there.

What we call psychic sensitivity is not a supernatural gift bestowed on a chosen few. It is a neurological capacity. The developed ability to receive and interpret subtle information that most people in modern Western culture have never been trained to notice, and in many cases have been actively trained to ignore. When someone cultivates genuine psychic sensitivity they are doing something neurologically specific. They are rewiring neural pathways to accept information that does not arrive through the five ordinary senses. The brain is an active filter, constantly making decisions about what information to pass through to conscious awareness and what to discard as noise. Those filtering decisions are shaped by experience, by expectation, and most powerfully by cultural permission. What a culture tells you is real determines, to a remarkable degree, what your brain allows you to consciously perceive.

The tools that sensitives use, tarot cards, divination rods, pendulums, automatic writing, candles, ritual objects of every tradition, are not the source of the information. They are training mechanisms. The tool focuses the attention. The focused attention develops the neural pathway. The developed neural pathway becomes increasingly capable of interpreting the signal without the tool. It is the same mechanism as stroke rehabilitation, where new neural pathways route around damage to accomplish the same function through different means. Directed toward developing sensitivity to subtle environmental signals, the same plasticity produces the same result.

Children, before cultural training takes hold, perceive with a freedom and openness that most adults have long since lost. The young brain in extraordinary neuroplasticity, the filters not yet built, the cultural vocabulary not yet fully installed, is capable of perceiving things the adult brain has been trained to screen out before they reach conscious awareness. The phenomenon of the imaginary friend deserves far more serious examination than it typically receives. Some of what children describe with that label may not be imaginary at all.

This capacity exists across every culture on earth, but what varies enormously is whether that culture gives people permission to develop it, language to work with it, and a community to help them do so safely.

In Umbanda, the Afro-Brazilian spiritual tradition I had the privilege of working within, every priest and priestess is trained from the beginning to become a medium. It is not a rare calling. It is the path. Over years of practice and guidance they develop the capacity to minister to their congregation one person at a time, perceived presences becoming a tool of healing rather than a source of terror. The tradition assumes the capacity is real and builds an entire structure around developing it responsibly.

Kardecism, founded by the French educator Allan Kardec in the nineteenth century and now practiced by tens of millions across Brazil, opens people to the spiritual dimensions of life as a matter of daily faith rather than exceptional experience. In Brazil you can walk into a Kardecist center in almost any city and find ordinary people sitting together, developing their perceptions, sharing what they receive, comparing it against each other for accuracy. The capacity is not treated as strange. It is treated as something to be cultivated, like any other skill.

In Thailand, spirit houses stand at the entrance of nearly every home and business in the country, small ornate structures where daily offerings are made to the presences that share the space. The boundary between the living and the dead is understood as permeable and navigable. Spiritual awareness is woven into the rhythm of daily life rather than segregated into churches or dismissed as superstition.

These are not primitive traditions that the modern world has left behind. They are sophisticated systems developed across centuries for working with a capacity that the Western world has spent just as many centuries trying to eradicate.

Because that is the other side of this story, and it is one I have witnessed firsthand across Latin America and beyond. Throughout much of the world, and especially in Catholic countries, people who perceive what others cannot are not celebrated or guided. They are labeled. The word most commonly applied to them is witch. The response most commonly offered is exorcism. A child who sees things others cannot, a woman who senses presences in rooms before anyone else does, a man whose anxiety generates phenomena in his immediate environment, these people have learned through painful experience to hide what they are. The Church that brought rituals designed to help people trapped by genuine phenomena also became the institution that condemned the very perceptual capacity it would need to verify those phenomena were real.

Chris McKinnell with Archbishop Cristian Piedrahita Montoya and Isabel Goyeneche during an investigation of a haunted bordello and strip club in Bogota, Colombia. The case is a reminder that paranormal phenomena do not confine themselves to places we consider sacred.

I have sat across from women in Latin America who carry this wound. Women who have spent their entire lives hiding what they perceive, afraid of what their community would say, afraid of what the Church would say, afraid of themselves. My connection through my grandparents to the Conjuring universe of films means that in cultures where the paranormal is otherwise taboo, people feel safer bringing me what they have carried alone for years. Watching a woman break down in tears because she has finally found someone who understands and accepts what she is, is both heartbreaking and beautiful. Heartbreaking because of how long she carried it alone. Beautiful because she no longer has to.

The foundation my grandmother Lorraine and I started together in 2013 grew out of exactly that need, a flood of people reaching out after the first Conjuring film, finally having a name they recognized to attach to experiences they had carried in silence. What walks through that door is not a ghost story. It is a person who needs to be told that there is nothing wrong with them.

My grandfather's story begins at exactly this same place.

Ed Warren was a child in an ordinary household when he first encountered something he had no rational means of explaining. A middle-aged woman appeared in his bedroom. She sat on his bed, introducing herself as Babe. She spoke to him kindly. His family dismissed it. But the experience was specific enough that he described the woman in detail to his father, including things about her appearance that no one had told him. His father recognized her from the description. She was Ed's aunt, who had died before he was born.

A child in a skeptical household described someone he had never met, in accurate verifiable detail, confirmed by the one person in the family who would have recognized her. That single encounter set Ed Warren on the path he followed for the rest of his life. The entire Warren legacy traces back to that moment. The capacity was always there. What changed was the moment it could no longer be ignored.

There is a question I am asked more often than almost any other, and it is a genuinely good one.

How does a spirit that has never encountered our technology know how to use it?

I want to tell you what I think is actually happening, based on decades of observation, and I want to start with something that happened in my own hands.

My grandmother died on a spring evening in April, 2019 while I sat beside her. I had my iPad with me. At the precise moment she passed, the battery drained from thirty-five percent to zero. Not gradually. Immediately. As though something had reached into the device and taken what it needed on the way out.

I have seen this pattern hundreds of times in this work. Psychics flickering lights or turning TVs on and off without touching them. Cell phone batteries draining in seconds in the presence of certain people or in certain locations. I worked with a woman in Surrey, England, who could not hold a phone long enough to speak with me. She suffered from severe anxiety and agoraphobia, and she and her daughter were both extraordinarily gifted. We ran a simple experiment. Her mother held the phone and we spoke normally. Then she took the phone, and it dropped the call immediately. Her energy interacting with the device shorted it out every time. Her mother's did not.

What this tells me is something straightforward once you accept the premise that consciousness is fundamentally energy. Spirits are energy untethered from physical form. And energy manipulation, which sounds dramatic when you say it that way, is actually the simplest and most natural thing available to them. It requires no fine motor control, no physical infrastructure, no understanding of how the device on the receiving end actually works.

Think about how you speak. Air moves through your vocal cords in ways you have never consciously studied and could not accurately describe. You simply intend to speak and it happens. The mechanism is invisible to you because you have never needed to see it. I believe something similar is true of how consciousness without a body interacts with the physical world. The intention is there. The energy finds its way through whatever channel is available. The spirit is not operating the technology. It is moving through it the way water moves through whatever container it finds.

This explains something that has always struck me about the history of these communications. Throughout much of the 20th century people reported telephone calls from the dead, hearing a loved one's voice on a live line with no explanation. There were cassette players recording ghostly voices that answered questions in graveyards or seances. Then it was voices on answering machines. Then text messages from phone numbers that had been disconnected for years. Then emails. Now EVP recordings, spirit boxes, digital voice recorders. The technology changes with every generation. The phenomenon does not.

A consciousness from the nineteenth century has never seen a cassette recorder. It does not need to understand the device any more than the device needs to understand it. Something is trying to reach someone, the energy moves toward the nearest available channel, and what comes through takes the shape of whatever that channel produces.

What varies enormously is the degree of control behind it.

At one end of the spectrum you have what I think of as the uncontrolled release, raw energy finding the path of least resistance with no precision behind it. The lights flicker. The battery drains. Glass shatters. A bed lifts off the floor and travels across the room. These phenomena are dramatic precisely because they are undirected, more like a pressure valve releasing than a hand reaching out deliberately. Nobody planned the broken glass. Nobody aimed the bed. The energy simply went somewhere.

At the other end of the spectrum you occasionally see something that looks much more like actual intention. A photo of a loved one who has just passed falling to the floor. A set of keys goes missing. You search everywhere. Two hours later they are sitting exactly where you already looked, in plain sight, as though they were always there. That is not an explosion of uncontrolled energy. That is something small, moved deliberately, and returned. Whatever produced it had enough focus to place an object and enough patience to wait. That kind of precision is rare, and when you encounter it, it deserves a different kind of attention than the shattering glass.

And then there is a third category, the one that stays with me longest. The communication that is not only intentional but considerate.

When I first moved to San Jose, Costa Rica, a woman approached me whose mother was dying of cancer. Her mother was terrified of death and wanted to know what waited on the other side. My Spanish was not strong enough at the time to have that conversation directly, so I found a translator and sent word that I would be able to speak with her mother the following day.

I did not hear back.

That night at two in the morning my television turned on by itself. It switched from my Amazon Fire Stick menu to YouTube and began playing a Spanish love song. Two people on screen, clearly in love, singing to one another. I could make out enough of the words to understand what it was. I assumed it was something that had followed me home from a haunted sanatorium called Sanatorio Duran, which I had visited that same day, and I told it plainly to leave. It did.

Two hours later I woke again, curious about the song. I went to my iPad and opened my YouTube account to look at the viewing history.

There was nothing there.

The playback had occurred. I had watched it. But there was no record of it in the account history, while everything else I had watched remained exactly where it should be. If you have ever used a streaming service you know that it records everything, automatically, without exception. The only explanations are that someone accessed my account and deleted that single entry while leaving everything else intact, which makes no sense at all, or that whatever produced the playback did not produce it through the ordinary mechanism that generates a history entry in the first place.

The next morning I turned on the television and another Spanish love song was playing again on YouTube. I had closed the application the night before. I couldn't imagine at the time what was going on.

That afternoon I received a message from the woman's daughter. Her mother had died during the night.

What became clear to me as I sat with that is something I have thought about many times since. Her mother had not sent that love song to her daughter. She had sent it to me. A television turning on by itself in the middle of the night would have terrified her daughter. She knew that. She also knew, apparently, that it would not terrify me. So she reached the person who could receive it without fear, so that the message of love could be passed on to the person who could not. I was not able to give the daughter the specific song her mother had chosen. That is the one thing I wish I could have given her and could not. But I was able to tell her that her mother had come through, that she had found a way to say what she needed to say, and that the last thing she did before she left was send love.

That is not a random energy discharge. A random energy discharge does not make that calculation. It does not consider who will be frightened and who will not, does not choose the messenger, does not wait until the right moment and then find exactly the right channel. What her mother did required intention, awareness of the people involved, and what I can only describe as care.

Chris McKinnell with Alma Rayas during an investigation tour of Mexico. Alma led the team that would bring Chris to the ruins above San Jose, Costa Rica, where one of the most striking cases of documented post-death communication he has ever encountered took place.

The technology keeps changing. That quality of care does not.

And sometimes the intention is specific enough, and the connection strong enough, that what comes through carries information nobody else could have known.

I worked a different case around 2021 involving a woman in Mexico City whose mother had died. She began receiving text messages that she shared with me, from a defunct account, warning her that her brother was in danger and that she needed to look after him. She did not know how to receive what was being sent. She did not know how to act on it. Shortly afterward her brother was killed.

And then he contacted her. Through the same channels his mother had used. He told her he was fine. He told her she should not carry guilt for what she could not have prevented.

I am telling you this not as a ghost story but as a data point. A warning was delivered before an event. The event occurred. A message of reassurance followed. The same family. The same channel. Two separate consciousnesses using whatever mechanism was available to reach someone they loved.

The technology is not the point. It never was. The point is the intention behind it, and the love that makes that intention strong enough to find a way through.

I want to say something plainly about what happens when that capacity is met not with understanding but with exploitation, because I have watched it cause real harm to real people and I am not willing to stay quiet about it.

Watching a paranormal reality program or a YouTube investigation and deciding you are qualified to walk into someone's home and assess what they are living with is the same thing as watching Grey's Anatomy and deciding you can perform surgery. The entertainment industry that has grown up around this work exists to generate fear, because fear generates ratings. It does not exist to help anyone understand what is actually happening in their home. What it teaches people about this field is not investigation. It is theater. And when frightened people invite that theater into their most vulnerable moments, the consequences can be devastating.

I worked with a woman in Florida years ago who had reached out to a team of self-described paranormal investigators after experiencing activity in her home. They arrived with their equipment and their cameras. Their psychic walked through the house, announced that she was dealing with a Lilith demon, and the entire team ran out saying they weren't qualified to handle something like that. They left her alone with that label and no tools to address it. I wish I could say that was an isolated incident, but it is very common.

She was not dealing with a demon. She was a psychically gifted woman suffering from anxiety who had never been taught to ground her energy. The activity in her home was a direct expression of what was running unmanaged through her own awareness. Once we identified what was actually happening and gave her the tools to work with it, everything changed. But before that happened she had spent months driving from Florida to Georgia every month, paying six hundred dollars from her pension for a deliverance service she never needed. Six hundred dollars a month. Because someone named a monster and ran.

A man from Pakistan living in London came to me after years of paying a practitioner back home who had told him a curse was responsible for his physical ailments. There was a payment required to address it. And then another payment to maintain the remedy. And then another. He had real medical issues that deserved real medical attention and these supposed treatments weren't actually helping. But he had also been told that stopping the payments would cause the symptoms to growing worse, which meant the practitioner had every incentive to ensure the problem never fully resolved. That is not spiritual work. That is the deliberate cultivation of dependency. It is the oldest exploitation available, fear maintained because fear pays.

I have never charged a family for assistance and I never will. Not because I cannot use the money. Because the moment you charge someone for their fear you have made yourself part of the problem rather than the solution. Anyone who tells you otherwise is not doing this work for the right reasons.

The first thing I tell anyone dealing with activity in their home is to turn off the paranormal programs. Stop feeding the fear with images and frameworks designed to make everything look as threatening as possible. You are not learning anything from those programs. You are being conditioned to be afraid of something that in the vast majority of cases does not deserve your fear and is made significantly worse by it.

The gifts we are born with, the ones this chapter has been describing, the ones that exists in varying degrees across every human population on earth, deserves to be met with understanding, discipline, and genuine care. Not cameras. Not labels. Not monthly payments to someone whose income depends on your continued suffering.

The problem is not the phenomena. The phenomena are real. The problem, as I got wrong myself for the first several years of my work, is the label.

My grandparents did not begin their investigations as demonologists with a fully formed theological framework. They began as investigators, two people from working-class Catholic backgrounds in Connecticut who kept encountering things they could not explain. When the phenomena exceeded what ordinary categories could hold, they reached for what they knew. Their faith. Their tradition. The vocabulary that Catholicism provided for encounters with the deeply disturbing and the genuinely threatening. Over decades of investigation they adapted, changed their understanding as the evidence demanded it. By the end of my grandfather's life his understanding of what he was dealing with was considerably more nuanced than the one he had started with.

Religion is a remarkable tool for this work. A Catholic exorcism performed with full commitment can produce real results. So can a Kogi ceremony. So can the work of an Umbanda priest-medium in Brazil. Different vocabularies, different symbols, different theological structures, consistent results when the practitioner brings focused intention to the work.

Chris McKinnell with members of the Kogi people in the Sierra Nevada de Santa Marta, Colombia. One of the last intact pre-Columbian civilizations on earth, the Kogi's understanding of consciousness and the interconnection of all things has informed Chris's investigative framework for decades.

Religion is a great tool for dealing with these phenomena. It is a poor framework for examining them.

A tool addresses the situation. A framework decides in advance what the situation is. When you enter an investigation carrying a predetermined explanation, you are not investigating. You are confirming.

Understanding where the most powerful of these labels comes from is essential to seeing past it.

The word demon comes from the ancient Greek daimon. In classical Greek understanding the daimon was not an evil being. It was an intermediary, a spiritual presence that existed between the gods and humanity, capable of being benevolent, harmful, or neutral. Socrates famously described his own daimon as an inner voice that warned him away from harmful actions. The Romans carried this understanding forward, expanding it to include the genius, the divine animating power that expressed itself through a person's particular gifts and capacities.

As Christianity spread through the Mediterranean world it encountered existing religious traditions with their own gods, spirits, and sacred practices. The theological strategy employed was straightforward and devastatingly effective. The gods and spirits of other traditions were not dismissed as fictional. They were reclassified as evil. Beelzebub was originally a Philistine deity, worshipped with genuine reverence. Pazuzu, famous as the antagonist in The Exorcist, was originally a protective presence. Pregnant women wore his amulets around their necks to ward off the demoness Lamashtu, who was blamed for miscarriages and infant deaths. Pazuzu was protection. The later tradition made him the horror.

In the Hebrew Bible, in the Book of Job, the figure known in English as Satan bears almost no resemblance to the cosmic villain of medieval Christian theology. The original Hebrew term is ha-satan, a title, not a proper name. It means the adversary, or more precisely, the prosecutor. Ha-satan appears in the divine court as a subordinate of God, performing a function the court apparently requires. He tests. He challenges. He is not in rebellion against God. He is working within the divine structure. The leader of an army of fallen angels locked in eternal opposition to God did not exist in this text. That character was assembled gradually across centuries, built from fragments of different traditions into a mythology of cosmic evil. The transformation was not driven by evidence. It was driven by the institutional need for a sufficiently powerful enemy.

In 1597 a Scottish king named James VI wrote a book called Daemonologie to prove the existence of witchcraft and justify the hunting and execution of those who practiced it. When he later commissioned the Bible translation that bears his name, a consequential change appeared in the text. The original Hebrew phrase referring to someone who used herbs or compounds to harm others became thou shalt not suffer a witch to live. One man's fear, encoded into scripture, became theological justification for the execution of thousands of people across Europe and the American colonies. Many of those people were not practicing anything dangerous. They were simply perceiving things others could not, in a culture that had decided the only explanation for that was diabolical.

The label was not the reality. But the label had the power of a king and the authority of holy text behind it.

My grandparents worked within the framework that history had produced, with courage and care and a commitment to the people they were trying to help. What my grandfather gave me was not a theology. It was a methodology. Document everything. Take the experience seriously. Follow the evidence wherever it leads and do not stop at the label.

Every tradition, from the Animists of Mali to the Umbanda priests of Brazil to the Buddhist monks of Thailand to the Catholic mystics of medieval Europe, is using a different vocabulary to point at the same thing. Something larger than any single framework can contain. Something that existed before the first label was attached to it and will exist long after the last one has been forgotten.

A child who sees things others cannot is not ill, not diabolical, not in need of exorcism. They are picking up signals that have always been there. The question that remains is what those signals are actually made of, and what it means that they can be generated not only by the dead reaching toward the living, but by the living shaping their own reality through the quality of what they hold in mind.

That is where we are going next, and it begins with a Raggedy Ann doll in Hartford, Connecticut.

IX. ANNABELLE COMES HOME

The doll arrived as a gift.

Donna's mother had found it in a second-hand store in Hartford and thought it would make a nice housewarming present for her daughter and her roommate, two young nursing students setting up their first apartment together. It was a Knickerbocker Raggedy Ann, three feet tall, with the friendly stitched face that generations of American children had grown up loving. Cheerful. Harmless-looking. The kind of thing you put in the corner of a room and it makes the room feel inhabited.

The girls loved it immediately. They sat it at the table when they ate. They took turns sleeping with it. They talked to it the way you talk to something you have decided to love. They named it Annabelle.

This was 1969, the age of Aquarius, a moment when young people were genuinely open to the possibility that the universe was alive and communicating. When the doll's arms lifted themselves onto the breakfast table one morning, the girls were intrigued rather than frightened. They assumed there was a spirit in it. They called a medium.

Over a series of sessions, the medium came to believe she was receiving messages from a little girl named Annabelle Higgins. The child had been killed by a car in front of the house, she told them. She was lonely. She just wanted someone to love her.

The girls were already attached to the doll. They already wanted to believe it was something that needed their care. The medium gave that desire a name, a history, and a face. They poured everything into it. They took the doll everywhere. They bought it clothing and a bracelet that is still around its wrist today. They talked to it like a child who needed comforting and protecting.

And something responded.

It moved through the apartment the way a playful child might. It appeared in different rooms when they came home. Notes appeared on parchment paper in a childlike hand. "Miss me?" "Wanna play"? The phenomenon reflected back exactly what it had been given: love, attention, and the shape of a lost child who wanted to belong.

Then something shifted. Not in the doll. In the girls.

The activity that had delighted them began to unsettle them. The sense of being watched crept in. Lights flickered. Something knocked inside the walls. What had felt like wonder began to feel like threat. And the phenomenon responded to that shift with the same fidelity it had shown from the beginning. It gave them back what they were putting in. Their fear had replaced their love, and the thing they had built was not distinguishing between the two. It was amplifying whichever one arrived.

The final note was different from the others. Not playful. Not curious. "Help me."

Donna's boyfriend had never trusted the doll. He begged her to let him burn it. One afternoon he fell asleep on the couch and woke from a dream that Annabelle was on top of him, strangling the life out of him. Whether that was a dream responding to his hatred of the thing, or the thing responding to his hatred of it, is a question I leave open. What is documented is what happened when he stood up, walked across the room, picked the doll up, told it that it was just a dumb doll and could not hurt anyone, and threw it across the room.

According to my grandfather, who investigated the case directly, the young man was immediately clawed seven times across the chest and abdomen, the wounds deep enough that blood soaked through his shirt. The walls hammered with invisible fists. The chair the doll had been sitting in came rocketing across the room.

They called the Episcopal Canon of Hartford. The Canon called his exorcist, Father Richard Nolan. Father Nolan called my grandparents.

My grandmother Lorraine felt it the moment she walked in. Not curiosity. Not the presence of a child who wanted company. Something heavy and oppressive that pushed back against her in a way she recognized immediately. Her Catholic faith gave her a name for that heaviness. She taught me that name, and for years when I walked into a home and felt that same quality in the air, I used it. I was twenty-six years old before I could no longer accept the label as an explanation. But that came later. On that afternoon in Hartford, my grandmother knew what she was feeling was not the spirit of a little girl named Annabelle Higgins.

My grandfather had already reached the same conclusion from a different direction. He could not reconcile the theology of a child's spirit attaching to a doll with the faith he held. He was a man working with the tools his tradition had given him, and within those tools he found what he needed: it was demonic and was removed from the apartment. The girls were never bothered again.

Annabelle came home with my grandparents.

I should tell you what I mean when I say I grew up with Annabelle, because it is not what most people imagine when they hear it. I am not afraid of it. I never have been. It has been part of my life for as long as I can remember, and what I feel in its presence is not terror. It is the particular alertness you feel around something that requires respect and knowledge. The way you feel near a downed power line. You do not panic. You do not pretend it is harmless. You give it exactly the distance and attention it deserves, and you keep moving.

My grandmother, one of the most gifted psychics I have ever known, avoided looking at the doll her entire life. I understood why. What I sensed in that room was never neutral. But growing up around it meant I understood what it was in a way that most people who encounter the Annabelle story never have the chance to.

After my grandparents brought the doll home, they had no immediate means of containing whatever had gathered around it. For years it sat in a rocking chair in the museum. Then one afternoon around 1975, our friend Father Bill Charbonneau came to visit. He was a young priest who had bought himself a new car and wanted to show it off to his two closest friends.

At some point the conversation turned to the doll. Father Bill had heard the stories. When they went downstairs to the museum, he walked straight up to it, looked at it, and announced: "God is stronger than the Devil." Then he threw Annabelle across the room, exactly as Donna's boyfriend had done six years earlier.

My grandfather looked at him with what I can only describe as resigned patience.

"Yes Father," he said. "God is stronger than the Devil. But no man is."

That night, driving home alone on Route 8, Father Bill saw a bright light descending from the sky straight towards his new car.

He veered to avoid it and crashed into the median strip, ripping the car in half. He miraculously survived with a broken leg. He told my grandfather afterward that in the halo of that light, he had seen Annabelle.

I have heard my grandfather give lectures over the years describing a young couple on a motorcycle who taunted the doll on their way out of the museum and died in an accident on the way home. I have never found any evidence that story is true. What I believe is that my grandfather changed the details to protect Father Bill's identity while still conveying what he felt was the essential lesson. Father Bill had asked him to keep his name out of it. My grandfather honored that. Now that Father Bill is gone, I am telling you what actually happened. I owe him that honesty, and I owe you the same.

Father Bill Charbonneau, a young priest and close friend of Ed and Lorraine Warren. His encounter with Annabelle on Route 8 left him with a broken leg and a story he asked my grandfather to keep private. He is gone now and wouldn't mind this being shared now.

After the accident on Route 8, my grandfather built the box that houses the doll to this day. Religious medals. A rosary. Blessed salt. A cross. Prayers sealed into the construction. A sign on the front that reads, positively do not open. My grandfather also had a flair for the dramatic, which is why the devil tarot card appears on the box alongside the religious objects. It was one more warning, dressed in his particular style. He intended the box to be permanent. The doll was never meant to be removed.

In 2024 and 2025, Annabelle went on tour.

I said publicly and clearly that I believed this was a serious mistake. The box was designed to contain something. It was not designed for public venues, for crowds of people with no understanding of what they were handling, for the kind of casual proximity that a traveling exhibition invites.

Dan Rivera was the man responsible for moving the doll during that tour. He described on the Ghost City Tours podcast what happened the first time he touched Annabelle without proper precautions: he drove to an intersection and was struck by vehicles coming from three directions at once. Dan Rivera died while on tour with Annabelle. I am not drawing a line between those two facts. He was a person, and his life was more than the way it ended. I find it difficult to look at this without wondering.

There have been other incidents across the years.

A homicide detective came to consult my grandmother on a case, not an unusual arrangement. The Monroe Police Department had always had a close relationship with my grandparents and occasionally asked for Lorraine's help. After their consultation, the detective asked to see the museum. My grandfather stepped away to take a call upstairs and told him to look around but not to touch anything. When he came back down, the museum looked as though a hurricane had passed through it, and the glass case protecting the public from Annabelle was standing open. The detective came up the stairs pale as chalk, refused to tell my grandfather what had happened, and agreed to tell my grandmother only if she promised never to repeat it. She kept that promise until her death.

On another occasion, my grandparents were driving through rural Pennsylvania on Route 84, passing through towns with biblical names, Bethlehem, Nazareth, Zion, Lord's Valley. My grandfather, in a moment of levity, remarked that not even Annabelle or the Amityville Horror could bother them in a stretch of road like that. The words were barely out of his mouth before their car was struck from behind with enough force to spin it off the road and into a ditch. A truck driver a quarter mile back stopped to help and told them it looked exactly as though another vehicle had hit them. There was no other vehicle.

My grandfather learned not to make fun of it.

Something happened around that doll in Hartford in 1969 that has not stopped happening in the more than fifty years since. Too many people across too many decades have encountered something in its proximity that they did not invent and had no reason to want. The Knickerbocker Raggedy Ann sitting in its box in Connecticut is not dangerous because it is evil in any simple sense of that word. It is dangerous the way certain forces are dangerous: not because they intend harm, but because most people have no idea what they are actually dealing with.

What were two nursing students in Hartford actually building when they poured their love and then their fear into that doll? What exactly gathers when human attention and emotion focus on something long enough and with enough intensity? What is the nature of the force that sent Father Bill's car into a median on Route 8, that clawed seven wounds across a young man's chest, that threw a decorated police detective up a flight of stairs in Monroe, Connecticut?

Those are not rhetorical questions. They have an answer. And that answer changes everything about how you understand not just Annabelle, but the nature of consciousness itself.

X. MANIFESTING REALITY

The nursing students did not summon a demon. They built one.

What gathered around that Raggedy Ann doll in Hartford was not an ancient malevolent intelligence descending from some external darkness. It was assembled piece by piece from the most human materials imaginable: love, attention, fear, and the sustained focus of two young women who had no idea what they were actually doing.

Peter Bancel, chief analyst for the Global Consciousness Project, conducted a rigorous seventeen-year review of data collected from random number generators placed around the world. The project had been designed to test whether major events drawing collective human attention produced measurable anomalies in the output. What Bancel found was not what anyone had anticipated. The anomalous effects had nothing to do with global events. They were associated with the researchers themselves. The people in the room who genuinely cared about the outcome, who brought focused attention to what they were measuring, were the ones producing the effect. Not a diffuse planetary field. Not the accumulated weight of shared tragedy or celebration. Specific people. Directed awareness. The difference between passive observation and genuine investment turned out to be the entire mechanism.

The Byrd study at San Francisco General Medical Center produced the same finding from a completely different direction. Cardiac patients were prayed for under rigorous double-blind conditions. Neither the patients nor their physicians knew who was receiving prayer. The patients who were prayed for showed statistically measurable improvements in their outcomes. A later and larger study, the STEP study, used scripted prayer delivered by strangers working from a structured protocol. It produced no benefit and a slight decline. The difference between the two studies was not the prayer. It was whether the person praying actually cared about the specific individual they were praying for. Genuine focused attention produced a measurable effect. Performed ritual without personal investment produced nothing.

I have seen this same pattern in every tradition I have worked within across more than forty years of field investigation. A Catholic exorcism performed with full commitment produces results. So does a Kogi ceremony. So does the work of an Umbanda priest-medium. The words differ. The symbols differ. The theological frameworks could not be more different from each other. What does not differ is this: when the practitioner brings genuine focused intention to the work, something happens. When they do not, nothing does. The ritual is not the mechanism. The ritual focuses the mechanism. The consciousness is what actually does the work.

When someone raises the placebo effect as a reason to dismiss all of this, they have made an error worth addressing directly. The placebo effect is not evidence against consciousness shaping reality. It is evidence for it. A sugar pill that produces genuine pain relief, measurable reduction in inflammation, and altered brain chemistry does so through belief alone. The body changed. Physiologically. Demonstrably. Not metaphorically. A person who believed they were receiving treatment produced real biological changes in their own body through the quality of their expectation. The question is not whether consciousness can produce physical effects. The placebo effect proves beyond any reasonable dispute that it can. The question is how far that capacity extends beyond the individual body of the person doing the believing. That is the genuinely open question. And it is exactly the question the nursing students in Hartford answered without knowing they were running the experiment.

Jesus said that faith the size of a mustard seed can move a mountain. That statement has been treated for centuries as a poetic expression of devotion. It is a precise description of a mechanism. Focused belief, intention channeled through genuine faith toward a specific outcome, produces tangible results. The size of the faith is less important than the quality of its focus. What the Byrd study measured in a hospital cardiac ward, what Bancel's researchers produced in a laboratory in Princeton, what every effective ritual across every tradition demonstrates in practice, is the same thing Jesus was describing on a hillside two thousand years ago.

This may account for more than we have been willing to consider. The apparitions of holy figures reported across centuries and across every major religious tradition, the miracles witnessed and documented by people with no reason to invent them, the interventions that arrive precisely when faith reaches a kind of critical intensity, these may not require an external supernatural source to be real. The mechanism may be us. Consciousness focusing itself through devotion and genuine need until it produces something that could not have arrived through ordinary means. That does not make the miracle less. It makes the capacity of consciousness more.

The inverse is equally instructive. When that same quality of human energy is present but not focused, when it is raw and undirected and sustained over time, it does not produce controlled results. It produces phenomena that nobody planned, that nobody can predict, and that nobody knows how to stop. The nursing students in Hartford were not trying to build something dangerous. They were running an enormous amount of emotional energy through a single focal point with no understanding of what they were doing. What they got was exactly what unfocused collective intention produces: something real, something powerful, and something that eventually moved well beyond their ability to manage.

Years ago, I worked with a woman in the Midwest whose adult son was on the autism spectrum. When he was growing up with her they had a contentious relationship, and whenever their conflict peaked, objects would fly across the room. When he moved out, everything stopped. She contacted me believing he needed to be cured of his autism. I told her plainly that there was nothing paranormal happening and nothing to cure. People on the spectrum are often extraordinarily gifted in their perceptual sensitivity, and I have come to believe they may represent the next step in human evolution rather than a deviation from it. What was happening in her home was not supernatural. It was two people with a charged and unresolved relationship generating enough emotional energy to affect the physical environment around them. She told me that when he came to visit, things would start moving in the apartment before he even arrived. I asked whether they still fought. They did. I suggested family counseling. She later told me that once they worked on their relationship, the activity stopped completely.

The same mechanism appeared more recently when a young father came to me. He had an infant and a toddler daughter. He came from a line of women with significant gifts and had lived with spiritual experiences his whole life. He had learned to manage them until his two-year-old started being affected. His wife had watched a clock fly across the room when she was alone in the house. A stack of plates had flown across the kitchen. The little girl was terrified to take a bath or sleep in her own room. As we talked it became clear that he was struggling with anxiety and there was real tension in his marriage. I gave him the same guidance my grandmother had given me and that I had seen work consistently for decades. Make sure the home is clean and free of clutter. Let the space breathe and the energy move freely. Turn off the paranormal programs and the horror movies. Watch things that make you laugh. Listen to music that makes you want to sing. Work on the relationships in the home and bring the energy up deliberately. Do not feed what you want to stop.

They did not need a house blessing. Within two weeks he reported no more manifestations. He sent me a photograph of his daughter in the bath with a huge smile on her face.

He said it was the first time in months she had been happy to take a bath, the first time she had gone to bed in her own room without fear, and that night he was going to sleep beside his wife where he belonged. Everything has been quiet since.

I want to tell you about a night in Tewksbury, Massachusetts that I have thought about ever since, because it is one of the clearest demonstrations I have ever witnessed of exactly what I am describing here and it changed how I looked at this phenomena forever.

The Malerba case had come to us in 1984. Ray Jefferson was a fellow student at the University of Connecticut, someone I knew from my own dorm, and of everyone I could have asked to join me in this work, I chose Ray. He said yes without hesitation and proved himself extraordinary at it every time we went out together. He was a dear friend who has since passed, and I think of him often.

Ray and I had been sent to investigate a poltergeist in Tewksbury while we were simultaneously working the Maurice Theriault case. Objects were flying. Windows were breaking. One of the younger boys seemed more affected than any other, his personality shifting in ways that alarmed everyone around him. He was rushed to the hospital by ambulance at one point, appearing to be in the grip of something that looked like a psychotic episode. There was tremendous tension running through that family, the kind of underlying pressure I had not yet learned to look for as the source of what was manifesting around them.

The case had made the local newspaper after Lorraine Malerba called the police and the responding officers told her, in so many words, to stop reporting things that were not happening. When Ray and I arrived for our first visit the neighborhood roads were jammed with hundreds of cars. People were standing on the sidewalk outside the house, pressing forward, trying to get a look at something that had become a spectacle. I walked toward the crowd and I was not gentle about it.

"This is somebody's home," I yelled at them when they begged to be allowed in. "These are real people with real children and they are going through something terrible. Get the hell off the lawn!" I said as we walked up the porch steps, turning my back in them.

Over the following months Ray and I documented significant physical phenomena in the house. Father McKenna came in, performed a thorough spiritual cleansing, and everything stopped. The house went completely quiet. That was the same day, as it happened, that we conducted the Maurice Theriault exorcism in which my grandfather suffered a heart attack 10 feet away from me. My grandmother always believed it was the concentrated energy at Tewksbury that caused it, not Maurice. The exorcism may seem the obvious choice, but I have no reason to doubt my grandmother.

After the case closed, I stayed in touch with the Malerbas. A few years passed. I returned from two years in Africa and was working with a new colleague named John. He had heard about the Tewksbury case and wanted to meet the family. Lorraine invited us to spend the night.

The ten year old boy whose room we were borrowing was not pleased about sleeping on the floor. This is the same boy that was so deeply affected the first time we were involved. Nobody asked him how he felt about it.

That was a mistake.

We settled into our sleeping bags on the bed and turned off the light.

"Chris, stop kicking the bed." John thought I was trying to scare him.

I turned on the light and showed him I was lying completely still, wrapped tightly in my bag. He grumbled. He turned the light off again.

"Chris, stop kick…" he yelled.

The bed with both of us on it lifted about a foot off the floor, traveled ten feet across the room perpendicular to where the boy was lying, and crashed down in pieces.

I started laughing. I couldn't help it. The sheer impossibility of what had just happened, the speed and the sound and the violence of it, came out as pure astonished delight. I had never experienced anything like that. John immediately ran down the stairs.

When I caught up to him in the kitchen, Lorraine Malerba was sitting at the table with her back to us. She turned around, coffee in one hand, cigarette in her other, and looked at him.

"So," she said. "Ya believe me now?"

The house had been quiet for years before that night. It has been quiet in all the decades since. What broke the silence was not a demon that had been lying in wait, gathering strength, biding its time until the right moment. It was not a residual haunting suddenly reasserting itself. The cleansing had held. The only variable that night that I can identify was one small boy who had been displaced from his own bed without anyone thinking to ask how he felt about it, and who was quietly furious about it in the dark.

His unresolved emotion, in a space that had once held an enormous concentration of exactly that kind of energy, was apparently sufficient to lift two grown men off the floor and throw them across the room.

I cannot give you the precise mechanism. That is still part of the mystery that I am hopeful science will one day be able to answer. We are getting much closer to those answers every day. What I can tell you is what I observed, and what it pointed toward. The same pattern I keep seeing everywhere I look. Consciousness acting on physical reality through the quality of what it generates. Not supernatural. Not the work of an ancient intelligence with a name and a theology attached to it. Something operating at the intersection of emotion and matter in ways that should give anyone sitting comfortably inside a purely materialist framework genuine reason to pause.

A ten year old boy did not choose to throw that bed. He did not know he could. He was simply angry, in a space that remembered what anger felt like, and the energy went somewhere.

The question worth sitting with is not how unusual that is. The question is how often something like it is happening around us without the dramatic physical demonstration that makes it impossible to ignore.

A group of researchers in Colombia asked me something that has stayed with me. They wanted to understand why they were not seeing the same extreme, chaotic manifestations that are commonly reported in North America and Europe. Why did the phenomena in their experience seem more contained, more purposeful, less wildly destructive?

I have thought about that question for a long time and I believe the answer is this. In cultures that maintain living ritual traditions, whether that tradition is called Santeria, Brujeria, Umbanda, Candomble, or any of a dozen other names, the energy does not accumulate without direction. The ritual imposes focus. It channels what would otherwise run loose. A community that has practiced these disciplines across generations has developed, collectively, the same capacity that an individual develops through years of deliberate training. The energy is real in both cases. What differs is whether there is a structure to move it through. Where those structures exist, the manifestations tend to be purposeful. Where they have been lost or suppressed, the energy builds without discipline and eventually releases in ways nobody planned and nobody can control.

The poltergeist is almost always an unfocused phenomenon. Raw energy without direction. A household under emotional strain, a teenager in crisis, a relationship breaking apart at the seams, generating more than the physical environment can quietly absorb. The extreme manifestations we see in cultures that have lost their ritual traditions are not evidence that those cultures are more spiritually active. They are evidence that the energy has nowhere disciplined to go.

In 2023 I learned this lesson in a way I could not have anticipated and would not have chosen.

I was living in Paraguay with my daughter. One evening I reached over to turn on the lamp beside my bed and was electrocuted, thrown across the room by an invisible force. A few days later bruises the size of my palm appeared across my body, more than a dozen of them. I was racked with pain and could not walk. Doctors found no medical explanation for any of it. Objects were breaking throughout the house. My daughter and I were fighting constantly, which is not who we are with each other. I assumed I was having a run of bad luck and did not consider that anything deliberate was happening.

Then one Wednesday evening my grandmother Lorraine appeared to four separate psychics who did not know each other. She gave them all the same message. Chris is under attack. He needs to take this seriously. I woke to four messages waiting for me, texts and emails, all carrying the same warning from a woman who had been dead for years, delivered through four independent witnesses in a single night.

I took it seriously.

I performed a ritual bath to cleanse myself of any spiritual attachments and a thorough spiritual cleansing of the home. The pain stopped. The activity stopped. Immediately, not gradually. I was able to move again. The fighting between my daughter and me ceased as though it had never been there.

My belief is that the attack was connected to practitioners I had encountered through my work in 2023, people who understood how to focus energy with deliberate harmful intent. What some traditions call magic is what physics calls energy manipulation. The mechanism is the same one that produced measurable results in Bancel's laboratory and in the Byrd cardiac ward. Consciousness focused with genuine intention toward a specific outcome produces a tangible result. The intention in this case was not healing. And it worked, until a focused counter-intention arrived from a source that loved me enough to cross whatever distance death creates to deliver a warning in time.

Chris McKinnell during an investigation at a Masonic Temple in Asuncion, Paraguay. What presented as unsettling activity in the temple turned out to be the grandfather of the owner, who had simply never left. He was there to watch over his grandson and protect him. Not every presence is a threat. Sometimes love is the only explanation that fits the evidence.

My grandmother understood what I had not yet fully accepted about my own experience: that the same capacity which can bring a dying man's vital signs back from the edge of cardiac arrest can also throw a person across a room and leave bruises that no doctor can explain. The mechanism does not distinguish between the purposes it serves. We make those distinctions. And where we fail to make them deliberately, or where we direct that capacity toward harm rather than healing, the results are exactly as real as anything the Byrd study ever measured.

My grandmother knew this. The practical wisdom she passed on was not superstition. It was the accumulated understanding of someone who had spent decades watching the mechanism operate from both directions. Consciousness shaped by fear produces one reality. Consciousness shaped by love and genuine connection and the decision to choose light over darkness produces another. We are not passive witnesses to what manifests around us. We are its authors.

Every piece on the board is part of the same body. Every tentacle feeds back to the whole. What we generate individually and collectively, what we choose to focus on and sustain with our attention, becomes the world we inhabit together. The darkness and the light run on exactly the same fuel.

So the question that remains is not whether this capacity is real. The evidence for that is sitting in peer-reviewed journals, in the documented history of every living spiritual tradition on earth, and in the bruises that appeared on my body in Paraguay with no medical explanation and disappeared the moment I acted with conscious deliberate intention to remove what had been placed there.

The question is what you will do with it.

If consciousness focused through genuine intention can move the needle on a cardiac patient's recovery, build a thought form powerful enough to claw a man across the chest, carry a warning from a dead woman to four separate witnesses in a single night, and stop pain that no doctor could explain, then what you hold in your mind, what you feed with your attention, what you sustain with the quality of your daily awareness, is not a private matter. It is an act of creation. Every moment. Whether you intend it to be or not.

You are already manifesting your reality.

The only question worth asking is are you doing it consciously?

XI. THE TAPESTRY

There is a pattern running through everything we have covered so far, and it is time to say plainly what it is.

Every tradition we have examined arrives at the same recognition from a different direction. The Hindu understanding that the individual self, the Atman, is not separate from the universal consciousness underlying all existence but is that consciousness, temporarily experiencing itself as a distinct being. The Buddhist recognition that what we cling to as the permanent self is a construction. When Buddhism speaks of the absence of a fixed self it is not saying that you do not exist. It is saying that the self you defend so vigorously, the ego with its insistence on its own permanence and separateness, is not the deepest thing you are. It is the surface expression of something that was never actually separate from anything else. The Kogi and their Aluna, the invisible thought-world that precedes and generates physical reality, pointing toward the same understanding that what we see is the expression, not the source. The Egyptian reunification of the individual soul with its eternal origin after death. The Christian mystic's direct encounter with the divine spark within, that irreducible point where the individual and the infinite are the same thing. The Sufi poet's experience of the boundary between self and other finally dissolving, not as a loss but as a homecoming.

Different vocabularies. Different centuries. Different cultures with no contact with each other. The same recognition.

The apparent separateness of things is not the deepest truth about them. Underneath the experience of being a distinct individual moving through a distinct world is something that was never divided in the first place.

The Aboriginal Australians have maintained an unbroken living tradition for at least sixty-five thousand years. That is not a typo. Sixty-five thousand years of continuous cultural transmission, the oldest on earth by a distance that makes every other ancient tradition look recent. At the center of that tradition is what Western languages inadequately translate as the Dreamtime. It is not a creation myth. It is not a story about the past. The Dreamtime is the ever-present ground of being from which physical reality continuously emerges and to which it continuously returns. The ancestors are not gone. They are present in the landscape, in the living creatures, in the ceremonies that maintain the connection between the surface of existence and the depth underneath it. Every rock, every river, every living thing is a thread in a story that is always being told and never finished.

Sixty-five thousand years of people saying, with extraordinary consistency, that the membrane between the physical and the spiritual is not a wall.

Parmenides, the pre-Socratic philosopher writing in fifth-century Greece, arrived at the same recognition through pure reason alone. His argument was simple and radical. True being is one. It is singular, eternal, and unchanging. What our senses show us, change, movement, the apparent diversity of separate things moving through time, is not simply incomplete. It is structurally misleading. The only thing that actually exists is the one, undivided, without beginning or end. Everything else is what happens when perception tries to describe the one using instruments that were built for a different purpose.

He was largely set aside for centuries because the implications were too destabilizing for every system that followed him. You cannot build a theology or a political philosophy or a scientific methodology on the premise that the world of appearances is fundamentally misleading. So most traditions took what they needed from him and moved on. But what he was pointing at did not go anywhere. It kept reappearing, in Spinoza's single infinite substance he called God or Nature, in the holographic principle, in the block universe, in the near-death research where consciousness keeps demonstrating that it is not confined to the body or the moment the body inhabited.

In 2023, as I was actively formulating the framework this book is built on, I sat with a psychic whose work I have watched closely enough over the years to trust within the limits I apply to everyone, including myself. She was doing a past life reading, working through her particular pathway, which is visual art. She draws what she perceives. In that session she described what she believed were several of my past incarnations. A Mongol warlord, murderous and powerful. A Greek philosopher. Other lives as a wealthy man, other lives as a slave. She told me that in this lifetime my purpose is to learn about love and to share that understanding.

A representation of a Mongol warlord, believed to be a past life incarnation, drawn by the same psychic artist in Great Britain. Image Credit: Lana Grabowski

She described two figures she said were currently present as guiding influences. One was Pythagoras, whose name she recognized. The other she named as Parmenides. She had never heard of him. Did not know who he was. Had no framework for the name she was producing.

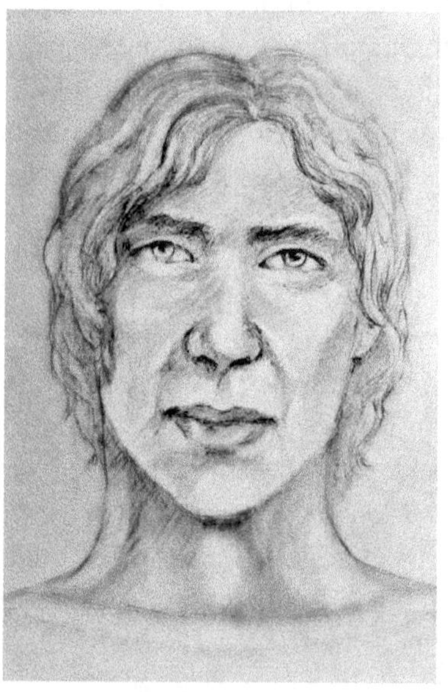

A portrait of Parmenides, identified as a guiding spiritual presence, drawn by a psychic artist in Great Britain without prior knowledge of his identity. Image Credit: Lana Grabowski

She produced a specific name from a tradition she had no knowledge of. I then researched that name independently and found a philosopher whose central argument, that reality is singular and undivided and that separation is a feature of perception rather than of truth, is the precise architecture of what I had been building in this book. The convergence is not something I can prove means anything. What I can say is that a consciousness organized around that particular understanding, if it persists and is drawn toward resonant work the way every other consciousness I have ever encountered seems to be drawn toward what it could not finish, would logically find its way toward someone currently engaged in exactly this argument. At exactly this moment.

That is worth noting. It is not worth overstating.

Parmenides represents an intellectual thread, a mind organized around the same architecture I had been building, drawn toward resonant work. What I want to tell you about next is something different in character, not a philosophical guide but a personal presence, someone whose connection to my family predates this book by decades.

Francesco Forgione was born in 1887 in a small village in southern Italy. He became a Franciscan friar and took the name Pio. In 1918 he received the stigmata, the wounds of the crucifixion, which he bore on his hands and feet for fifty years until his death in 1968. He was canonized by Pope John Paul II in 2002 and is one of the most extensively documented cases of sustained paranormal phenomena in modern history. Thousands of people reported encounters with him in locations far from his monastery while he was physically present there. The scent of roses or violets arriving without any visible source was consistently reported by people who prayed to him, both during his lifetime and after his death. He was investigated repeatedly by the Vatican, by skeptics, by physicians, and by journalists across decades, and the phenomena continued regardless of the scrutiny. He was also, by every account that survives him, genuinely funny. A man who bore open wounds in his hands and feet for half a century and could still make a pilgrim laugh.

There is a story about him that I love. A man made a long pilgrimage to meet Padre Pio, and every night along the way he prayed, Padre Pio, watch over my family and me. When he finally stood before him, he said it again. Padre Pio looked at him with great patience and said, my son, you have been saying that every night. Is there anything else you would like me to ask God for?

I consider him the patron of my family, and I say that as someone who does not identify as Christian and does not believe in saints in the institutional sense. I believe in consciousness that persists. I believe in love that does not require a heartbeat to remain active. And I believe that the man who was Padre Pio is still, by every measure I have ever used to evaluate these things, present and engaged and apparently possessed of an excellent sense of humor.

He has appeared in my family's story in ways that are independently documented. He appeared in a photograph taken at the Amityville house with my grandmother. My grandmother had been reading a biography of him the night she and my grandfather were first invited to Amityville, which may be coincidence and may be something else entirely. When I was investigating the home in West Pittston, Pennsylvania that became the basis for Conjuring Last Rites, I prayed to him and experienced what people across thousands of documented accounts have reported in his presence, the sudden unmistakable scent of roses in a room where there were no roses and no explanation.

And then, separately, a psychic who had never heard of him was given his name during a session and told me that he visits me often. She said he finds me amusing.

I choose to take that as a compliment.

The evidential structure is the same as everything else in this book. Specific detail. Independent confirmation. Followed by honest acknowledgment of what it does and does not prove. What it suggests, taken alongside everything else, is that the connections between consciousness do not dissolve when the body does. That attention, love, unfinished work, and genuine affection can maintain a thread between one awareness and another across whatever distance death creates. That the tentacle and the body are always in communication, and that the body includes everyone who has ever been part of it, on every side of the threshold we call death.

The information flows both ways. This is the part that most discussions of oneness miss, and it matters enormously for how we understand what genuine prayer, meditation, and psychic sensitivity actually are. When a person goes deeply still, when the noise of ordinary incarnated experience drops away long enough for something else to come through, they are not generating something new. They are opening a channel that was always there. What flows through that channel is not limited to what this particular consciousness has gathered in this particular lifetime. It is the accumulated experience of the whole, available to any tentacle that can quiet itself sufficiently to receive it. Parmenides working through a psychic who had never heard his name. Padre Pio answering prayers offered along a pilgrimage road before the pilgrim arrived. A great-grandfather appearing in the rearview mirror of a beat-up car on a rainy night because his granddaughter prayed for the boy driving it.

The same mechanism. The same direction of travel. Love and attention moving through a channel that was never actually closed.

There is a way of thinking about all of this that I find more comforting than any abstract argument, and it comes directly from the physics we established in Chapter Six. If every moment that has ever existed and every moment that will ever exist are equally real right now, if the flow of time is a feature of perception from inside the sequence rather than a feature of reality from outside it, then your great-grandparents are not gone in any absolute sense. They exist in the same eternal present as you do, in moments that are simply not the moment you are standing in right now. Your unborn great-grandchildren exist there too, living forward through a future that is as real and permanent as your present. The separations that feel so final from inside time, the deaths, the distances, the generations you will never overlap with, are features of the sequence. From outside the sequence they are simply different addresses in the same neighborhood.

Everyone you have ever loved still exists. Not as a memory. As a fact.

What we carry forward from previous incarnations is not always tender. Sometimes what persists is love that could not be expressed, reaching forward across the gap between lifetimes toward the connection it could not release. But sometimes it is not tender at all. Sometimes it is unresolved trauma, a wound that closed over without healing and keeps reappearing in a new life as a fear with no apparent origin in current experience, a pattern that keeps repeating, a grief that seems disproportionate to anything that has actually happened here. The curriculum is not always gentle. It is whatever remains unfinished, and what remains unfinished is calibrated precisely to what needs to be learned. The difficulties you carry may be doing exactly what they were meant to do. They are the forge. They are the material. What you do with them is the lesson.

The weaver and the tapestry and every single thread are the same thing. There is no outside vantage point from which the weaving is happening. The whole is doing it through every individual expression of itself, which means through you, right now, in this moment and every moment you inhabit.

We are not here to observe reality. We are here to participate in making it.

And what we bring to that participation, the quality of our connections, the willingness to see the other as an expression of the same source, the choice to lift rather than diminish, has consequences that extend considerably further than we can see from where we are standing.

Which brings us to the question that this entire architecture has been building toward. If the oneness is real, if the tapestry is complete and every thread is necessary, if the whole is already whole, then what exactly are we doing here? What does the curriculum ask of us? And what does it mean to love well inside a finite existence where the separation, though ultimately not the deepest truth, is also the only experience we have ever known?

XII. THE CHESS BOARD

I was not always the person writing these words.

I grew up in a home where love was real but the showing of it was hard. There was confusion in that house, and there was pain, and I spent most of my childhood trying to understand what I had done wrong. When I was fifteen I discovered something that changed the direction of my life, though I would not understand why for another forty years. I discovered that when I helped other people I felt accepted. It was not altruism. I don't believe in altruism. The father who gives his life to protect his child is doing it because any other choice would be inconceivable for him. That is not virtue. That is love expressing itself through the only action it can conceive of. For me, the mechanism was simpler and considerably less noble. I was a fifteen year old boy who had not felt wanted enough, learning that if he made himself useful to others they would keep him around. That was the beginning. Whatever it has grown into since, that was where it started.

Here is what I know from the other side of it. I am profoundly grateful for everything I went through. Not in spite of it. Because of it. The depth from which I am able to reach toward someone in darkness did not exist before the forge. And the thing I carry with me every day is this: I know I am not done. The learning does not stop. It should not stop. It should continue until the moment I stop breathing. That is not a burden. That is the whole point of being here.

So let us talk about the chess board.

Imagine one. Not a game between two opponents fighting for dominance. Something different entirely. A single awareness that has arranged the pieces with great care and deliberate intention, each one placed in exactly the position that will allow the game to unfold the way it needs to unfold. Every piece placed where it is for a reason. Every relationship between pieces considered. The configuration is not random. It is the product of a wisdom that understands what this particular arrangement is capable of producing.

And then the awareness steps back.

Not because the game no longer matters. Because the game can only work if the pieces move freely. A game where the outcome is predetermined by a hand moving the pieces from outside teaches nothing and produces nothing. A game where the pieces exercise genuine agency, where they struggle and adapt and choose and live with the consequences of those choices, that game has meaning. That game is the point.

The pieces are not playing against each other. They are dancing with each other. The relationships between them matter as much as any single piece's individual journey. Because every piece on that board is an expression of the same underlying awareness, temporarily separated into individual experience, encountering itself through every other piece on the board. The conflict between them is real. The love between them is real. The harm they do to each other is real. And all of it, every moment of friction and connection and loss and growth, is the whole becoming aware of itself in ways it could not become aware of from any single vantage point.

The circumstances you were born into were not random. The gifts and limitations you carry, the specific fears you arrived with, the relationships that were waiting before you got here, the wounds and the capacities that belong to you and no one else. These were arranged. Not to script the story before it began. Not to guarantee any particular outcome. But to create the conditions under which your particular expression of consciousness could encounter what it most needs to encounter. The board was set to make a certain kind of growth possible. What happens once the game begins is genuinely up to the pieces.

This brings us to the question that has occupied philosophers for centuries, the argument between free will and foreknowledge, and why that argument has never been satisfactorily resolved. It has not been resolved because it has been asked from inside the wrong frame.

Consider Benjamin Franklin. A time traveler who has studied his life in exhaustive detail goes back and watches him live it. The traveler knows every choice Franklin will make before Franklin makes it. He knows which experiments will be conducted, which political positions will be taken, which regrets will be carried to the grave. He has seen the whole story from the outside.

Does that foreknowledge change anything Franklin does? Does it reach back through time and cause his choices? Of course not. Franklin still wakes up every morning and makes every decision himself, freely, in the moment of making it. The traveler's knowledge is the view from outside the sequence. It is vision. It is not causation.

The awareness that set the board perceives all the moments of a lifetime simultaneously because from outside time the entire sequence is visible at once. That perception does not cause the choices made within it. The freedom is real. The foreknowledge is real. They are not in contradiction with each other. They only appear to contradict from inside linear time, looking forward at a future that has not yet arrived. From outside time both are simply two ways of describing the same reality from different vantage points.

Your choices are yours. The struggle is genuine. The growth that comes from it is earned.

You may reasonably ask, if the board was arranged with purpose and intention, if a consciousness wiser than our everyday selves set those conditions for growth, then what does that mean for the person whose life has included unbearable things? What does it mean for a parent watching a child suffer? What does it mean for anyone who has sat inside a darkness so complete that the idea of a purposeful universe felt like a cruel joke?

It means we have to look carefully at what the forge actually is, and what it is not.

A blacksmith takes raw ore, rough and unformed, and puts it to the fire. The heat is real. The hammer is real. The process is demanding and the ore does not choose it. But the blacksmith is not the ore's enemy. The fire and the hammer are not punishment. They are the process by which something raw becomes something of genuine strength and genuine use. The ore does not become the tool by being protected from the forge. It becomes the tool precisely because the forge was real.

Opposition is not the enemy of a good life. Opposition is the condition of one. A child whose every need is met before it arises has no reason to develop. No reason to reach or adapt or learn that other people have needs, that the world makes demands, that genuine care for another person costs something. We cannot truly comfort someone in grief if we have never grieved. We cannot understand what it takes to keep going if we have never been broken. The push and pull of genuine experience is not a flaw in the design. It is the design.

There is a difference between designed difficulty and human cruelty. One is part of the plan. The other is free will operating at its worst. And just because the chess master can see the layout of the game perfectly does not mean that every move on the board is controlled.

The forge is intentional. Abuse is not the forge. When a child is hurt by the person who was supposed to protect them, that is not a curriculum designed for their growth. That is a human being misusing the freedom they were given in a way that damages another. When a woman is violated by someone she trusted, that is not difficulty arranged for her benefit. That is cruelty. The pain it causes is real. The damage it does is real. Nothing I have said or will say is asking you to reframe that cruelty as a gift, or to find gratitude for surviving something that should never have happened to you.

The chess board was arranged with intention. But the pieces were given genuine agency. Real freedom. And real freedom means some pieces will choose to harm. You cannot have love without the possibility of its opposite. You cannot have courage without genuine danger. You cannot have compassion without the existence of suffering. The arrangement of conditions for growth is not the same as the arrangement of suffering itself. The first belongs to the chess master. The second belongs to the pieces, and specifically to the pieces that chose to misuse what they were given.

The grief you carry is real. The violation you survived is real. I am not asking you to love the person who harmed you. I am not asking you to decide that what happened to you was secretly good. What I am asking, eventually, is whether you might consider putting down the weight of carrying it into every subsequent moment of your life. Not for them. For you. There is an old story about a servant who carried water every day from a stream to his master's house, two clay pots hanging from a pole across his shoulders. One pot was perfect and arrived full every time. The other had a crack and leaked half its water along the path. The cracked pot was ashamed. It apologized to the servant one morning for its failure, for delivering only half of what a proper pot should. The servant smiled and pointed to the flowers growing along one side of the path. I knew about your crack from the beginning, he said. I planted seeds on your side of the road. Every day you have watered them without knowing it. Those flowers have fed this household and brought beauty to this table because of what you thought was only your flaw.

The crack is real. The flowers are also real. What you do with what broke you is the whole question.

I watched this truth walk beside me every day for years in the form of a woman named Clarice.

We met when we were both working as child abuse investigators and family therapists. The work takes something from you that most jobs do not ask for. You sit across from families at their absolute worst. You make decisions that alter the course of children's lives permanently. You carry what you have seen home with you because there is no clean way to leave it at the office. The people who last in that work, the ones who do not burn out or harden into something that cannot feel anymore, are usually the ones who have found a way to stay open to it without being destroyed by it.

Clarice had found that way. She was one of the most spiritually generous and genuinely empathetic people I have ever known. What I learned over time was that before we met she had been through addiction and a life on the streets that had taken her to places most people only encounter in case files. She had gone into rehabilitation against her will, meaning someone who loved her had insisted on it when she could not insist on it herself, and she had come out the other side transformed in a way that I do not think is too strong a word for.

What made her extraordinary at the work was not her training, though she was well trained. It was that when she sat across from a child who had been through something terrible, she was not reaching toward that child from a distance of professional sympathy. She was reaching from the inside of a shared experience. She knew what it felt like to be that child in that room. Not theoretically. In her body. In her history. And the children knew that she knew. You cannot fake that kind of recognition and you cannot manufacture it through any amount of education. It is what the forge produces when a person chooses to use what it made rather than be defined by what it cost.

The research supports what I observed in Clarice. Psychologists Richard Tedeschi and Lawrence Calhoun spent decades documenting what they called post-traumatic growth, the measurable increases in empathy, spiritual depth, appreciation for life, and genuine connection to others that consistently appear in people who work through severe adversity rather than around it. The suffering itself is not the cause of the growth. Working through it is. The distinction matters because it means the forge is not an argument for passively accepting what damages you. It is an argument for what becomes possible on the other side of it when you face it fully rather than flee it.

Clarice and I spent years doing exactly that, sitting with families in crisis, fighting for children who could not fight for themselves, trying to repair what could be repaired and protect what needed protecting. It was not comfortable work. It was not supposed to be. It was the board doing what the board was set for, putting people with particular histories and particular capacities in exactly the position where those histories and capacities were needed most.

Another truth that may startle you at first is one that I have come to accept with serenity.

Dying can be hard. Death is not.

For the living, death is loss. The grief is real, it deserves to be honored, and anyone who tells you otherwise has not loved someone enough. But understand what you are grieving. You are grieving yourself. You are grieving the absence of someone from your life. You are not grieving for them.

For the one who has passed, what felt so urgent from inside it, the striving and the losing and the loving and the wondering, resolves into something larger and quieter and full of recognition. Not ending. Return. A coming home to the larger whole from which we temporarily separated to make this journey.

A consistent pattern appears across every culture I have worked within. Spirits that do not pass immediately tend to linger anywhere from seven to forty days. They want to attend their own funerals. They check on the people they love. They want to make sure everyone is going to be all right before they go. This is not confusion. It is exactly what you would expect from a consciousness that has spent a lifetime in genuine connection with others. The love does not switch off. It completes itself.

What holds a consciousness in place beyond that window is the same thing that holds us in place during life. The unfinished. The unfaced. Guilt that was never acknowledged. Fear of what waits on the other side. A love so fierce it cannot let go, or a connection to a place too strong to release. Human beings are diverse in life and they carry that diversity with them. Free will does not end at death. If a consciousness does not want to pass over, it does not have to.

What waits on the other side is not judgment. It is the rest of the picture. The board does not stop being patient at the moment of death. What returns to the whole is not the ego that insisted on its own separateness. It is the awareness that was always underneath. Clearer now. Lighter. Carrying forward only what the long education has made of it.

Every piece on the board is part of something so much larger than any single game. Every thread of every life is being woven into a picture that no single piece, from where it stands inside the sequence, can fully see.

And this is where the question of what we owe each other becomes impossible to avoid. Because if the separation is ultimately an illusion, if every piece on the board is an expression of the same underlying awareness, then what we do to each other we do to ourselves. Not metaphorically. Literally. Which means the way we choose to move through the world, the quality of attention we bring to the people in front of us, the willingness to reach into darkness rather than turn away from it, is not just a personal virtue. It is the whole reaching toward itself through the only instrument available in this moment.

Which is you.

Right now.

In whatever moment you are reading this. The chapter you are in is not the whole book. But what you do with the chapter you are in is entirely up to you.

XIII. ALPHA AND OMEGA

There is a question that has been sitting underneath everything in this book, and it is time to look at it directly.

What was there before any of this began? And what remains when it ends?

Every tradition I have sat with, every discipline that has looked carefully at this territory, keeps arriving at the same place. Not similar places. The same place. The Hindu tradition calls it Brahman. The Aboriginal Australians call it the Dreamtime. The Kogi call it Aluna. The mystics of medieval Europe called it the ground of being. The physicists call it the unified field. The words are different. What they are pointing at is not.

There is no before. There is no after. There is only the one, and the one has no edges.

Think of a tapestry. Not one being assembled piece by piece, thread by thread, moving toward a completion that has not yet arrived. A tapestry that is already complete. Every thread that has ever been placed and every thread that will ever be placed is simultaneously present, the picture entire, nothing missing, nothing unfinished. That is the view from outside time and space. That is the vantage point of the All. That is what the traditions are pointing at when they speak of eternity, not an endless extension of time but the complete absence of it. A stillness that contains everything simultaneously because it exists in a dimension where sequence has no meaning.

That stillness is what we have chosen to call God.

Not a being who sits above creation making decisions about it. Not a judge keeping score or a father dispensing reward and punishment. The All itself. The eternal ground of being that is simultaneously the completeness of everything that has ever existed and everything that ever will. Alpha and omega not as the first and last letters of a story but as the paper the story is written on. The thing that makes the story possible at all, present before the first word and unchanged after the last.

Einstein demonstrated mathematically what the mystics had been saying for millennia. Time is not an absolute feature of reality. It is a feature of experience, specifically the experience of moving through the tapestry from inside it. From inside the weave, each moment arrives and passes and the sequence feels as real and solid as anything we have ever known, because from where we stand it is real. We are being woven into the tapestry as we move through it. Each moment of genuine love, each choice that costs something, each hand extended across the distance that the illusion of separation creates, is a thread being placed. The weaving is happening. The experience is not false.

But from outside time and space entirely, from the vantage point of the All, every moment is equally present. The child afraid in the dark and the old man setting down his last question are both there, equally real, equally held. The tapestry is already finished. We are being woven into it. Both of these things are true simultaneously, and there is no contradiction between them. There is only the difference between standing outside time and living inside it.

Outside time and space there cannot be cause and effect. There is simply oneness. A stillness. A completeness that has no before and no after because before and after belong to the experience of moving through time, not to what exists beyond it.

But that completeness is not a completeness despite the experience of creation. It is a completeness that comes from it. The All is not whole in spite of what we are going through down here in the weave. It is whole because of it. Every consciousness moving through a physical life, every fear faced and every love expressed and every lesson learned at whatever cost, is the All knowing itself from an angle that no other life can provide. We are not here despite the oneness. We are how the oneness knows itself fully.

This is not an abstraction. It has a shadow side that I have seen with my own eyes, and it has cost real people everything.

Maurice Theriault was a French-Canadian farmer who came to my grandparents for help in the early 1980s. Some readers will recognize the name from the Conjuring films, where the character called Frenchie carries it. The real Maurice was a man shaped by a childhood of savage abuse at the hands of his father, a man so brutal that his final act before taking his own life was to kill Maurice's mother while Maurice listened helplessly on the other end of a phone. Maurice came to us because something was tormenting him, and everything pointed toward his father as the source. Death had not softened him. Death had not humbled him. Whatever that man had been in life, he carried it with him when he left.

Standing at his father's grave, Maurice wept and told him he loved him and asked only that he find peace. What answered was a punch so hard it lifted him off the ground and threw him ten feet through the air. We all heard the impact. We all watched Maurice land flat on his back in the dirt, staring up at a sky that offered no explanation.

Maurice Theriault and his wife Nancy in a rare moment of peace during one of the most extraordinary cases of the Warren legacy. The real man behind the character called Frenchie in The Nun.

What I learned from that case, and from others like it across the years that followed, is that death does not automatically change a person. If someone spent a lifetime deeply invested in causing harm, that investment does not dissolve the moment the body does. The consciousness carries what it refuses to release.

This is the shadow the alpha and omega argument must account for. If the All is expressing itself through every individual life, then what are we to make of the lives that choose, consistently and deliberately, to move in the opposite direction of love? What happens to a consciousness so lost in the illusion of separation that it cannot conceive of the light as an option?

Those consciousnesses create their own darkness. Not as punishment imposed from outside. As the natural consequence of what they have chosen. A consciousness that spent a lifetime causing harm and never once turned toward accountability carries that weight into whatever comes next, and the weight itself becomes the prison. The darkness is self-generated. The isolation is self-sustaining. And from inside it, the light is not visible because the consciousness inside it has spent so long refusing to look in that direction that it has forgotten the direction exists.

This is what hell actually is. Not a place of external torment administered by a divine authority keeping score. A state of being generated from within, by a consciousness so invested in its own separateness, so far from the recognition of what it actually is, that it cannot find the door.

But the Umbanda tradition understands something about this that I have come to believe is true. There is no consciousness so damaged that the thread back is permanently severed. Fallen souls, those lost in their own darkness, can begin to find their way back through the act of service. By reaching toward others still more lost than themselves, something begins to open. The gesture of reaching toward another, even from inside genuine darkness, is itself a turning toward the light. In a timeless All, where every moment already exists simultaneously, the return of every apparently lost consciousness is not a hope. It is already woven into the tapestry.

There is no opposite of the All. There is only the All, and the degrees of distance from the recognition of what the All is. Evil is the All's most extreme forgetting. A consciousness so deep inside the experience of separation that it has lost all contact with what it actually is. The harm it causes is real. The darkness it generates is real. But it has no independent existence of its own. It is not a force equal and opposite to love. It is the absence of the recognition of love, the way darkness is not a thing in itself but the absence of light.

When you genuinely know, not as a philosophical position but as something felt in the body, that the person in front of you is the same consciousness wearing a different instrument, causing harm to them becomes incoherent. Not immoral in the rule-following sense. Incoherent. Like burning down your own house because you are angry at your neighbor.

That is what it means to approach oneness. Not a state of blissful detachment from the difficulties of the world. A state of recognition so complete that the illusion of separation, and everything that illusion makes possible including hatred and cruelty and the will to dominate, simply stops making sense as a choice.

We are not there yet as a species. The weave is still very much in progress. But the direction is not in question, because the tapestry is already complete and we are already in it. Every act of genuine love, every moment someone chooses connection over the illusion of separation, every hand extended across the distance that the forgetting creates, is not moving toward the All.

It is the All recognizing itself.

The alpha and the omega are not watching from a distance. They are what we are made of. The ground beneath every step and the awareness behind the eyes reading these words.

The only sane response to knowing what everything is made of is to treat it accordingly.

That is not a moral instruction. It is a description of what clarity actually looks like when the forgetting finally lifts.

XIV. WHY BOTHER?

If the tapestry is already complete, if the All is eternal and has never actually been divided, if every consciousness that has ever gotten lost eventually finds its way back to the recognition of what it always was, then a reasonable person sitting with all of that is going to ask a reasonable question.

Why bother?

If the destination is guaranteed, if the return is already woven into the fabric of what is, if even the most damaged consciousness eventually begins moving back toward the light, then what exactly is the point of the striving? Why try to be better than you were yesterday? Why extend yourself toward someone else's pain when the cosmic ledger is apparently going to balance itself regardless of what you do?

A student once went to a Zen master and asked what happens after enlightenment. The master said he chopped wood and carried water. The student was confused. But that is what you did before enlightenment, he said. The master agreed.

The tasks are the same. The person doing them is different.

The wood still needs chopping. The water still needs carrying. The question is who is holding the axe. Whether you are showing up for your own life or waiting for something external to make it feel worth the effort.

Nothing external will do that.

My grandparents worked a case involving an old man on Route 25 in Newtown, Connecticut, who had died and simply refused to leave his home. They tried mediation. They tried blessings. The old man was unmoved. He made life so miserable for the young family living there that they eventually fled. A sporting goods store moved in. It had to close as soon as the sun went down, or all hell would break loose. Eventually the property sold, the house was torn down, and a Pharmacy was built on the land.

The moment the house was gone, so was he. Not exorcised. Not blessed into submission. Released by the disappearance of the thing he was clinging to. He was not haunting the land. He was not haunting the family. He was haunting his home, the specific physical expression of what he refused to release. When that was gone there was nothing left to hold him.

We have the power to trap ourselves in what we refuse to release, to spend what could be living energy on what is already gone. The old man on Route 25 held on so tightly that even death could not open his hands.

For years I operated on the principle that I would trust people until they gave me a reason not to. I told myself this wasn't naive. I was honoring my principles. Looking back it was closer to a refusal to pay attention. I wanted to believe in people. I wanted to help. And so when something in me was already registering what I did not want to deal with, I found ways to explain it away. Not because I was foolish. Because acting on what I knew would have required me to act.

I had a young man living in my home. I was trying to keep him off the streets. I noticed my incense disappearing. I asked him about it more than once. He told me each time he had no idea where it was. He was burning it in front of me. I chose to believe the denial because acknowledging what I already knew would have meant doing something about it, and I kept finding reasons why the moment was not quite right.

That choice was mine. Everything that followed from it was mine.

I was in a wheelchair at the time. When I finally told him he needed to leave, he and his girlfriend threatened me with a knife. I was on the phone with the police when they beat me. They ran away laughing.

Choosing clearly, finally acting on what I had known for a long time, put me in genuine physical danger. It cost something real.

It was still the right decision. It has made all the difference.

I am grateful for everyone who has been in my life. I mean that without qualification. The ones who showed up and the ones who ran laughing. The ones who opened doors and the ones who held them shut. Every one of them offered me something, an opportunity to learn, to grow, to understand something about myself and about what I was willing to accept and what I was not. Some of those lessons were extraordinarily hard. Some of those people were painful beyond what I knew how to carry at the time.

But here is what I know. If I were living in the gutter today, I might not be so generous about it. The gratitude is not something that descended on me from outside. It came from choosing to take control of my own life. That is what made the gratitude possible. Not the suffering itself. What I chose to do with it.

People say they are powerless. They point to their circumstances, their diagnosis, their history, the things that were done to them that they did not choose and could not prevent. And sometimes the circumstances are devastating. Michael J. Fox has Parkinson's disease. Christopher Reeve spent years in a wheelchair after a riding accident that ended the life he had built. And arguably both of them did more for the world after those things happened than before. Not in spite of what they were facing. Because of what they chose to do while facing it. They did not let circumstance take away their power. That choice is available to anyone willing to make it.

The difference between I can't and I won't is the whole thing.

I can't hands the authorship of your life to your circumstances, your history, your fears, anything outside yourself that can be blamed for the shape things have taken. I won't is a decision. It is the acknowledgment that a choice exists and that you are making it. One of those statements is almost never actually true, and we all know which one when we stop pretending otherwise.

Consequences are real. We have to look at them honestly when we are making our choices. The knife and the beating were real consequences of a real decision. But the consequences of not choosing are also real. The consequence is living inside a reality you had the power to change and spending your life explaining why you couldn't.

Loving someone and keeping them in your life are not the same thing. There are people I love genuinely who are not part of my daily life. Some because the connection was pulling us both in the wrong direction. Some because they chose a different path. Letting them go did not end the love. It honored it. You can release someone from your story with complete genuine care for what they were in it and complete clarity that they cannot be part of what comes next. That is not hardness. That is the most mature form of love available to us.

We are the authors of our own lives. Not the authors of everything that happens to us. Some of what happens is the board being set, the conditions arranged, the forge doing what the forge does. But the authorship of how we meet it, what we make of it, whether we hand our power to it or use it as material, that is ours completely. I learned that from a wheelchair, from a knife, from two people running away laughing, from the quiet that followed when I understood the story was not over and that I was holding the pen.

Rumi knew what he was saying when he wrote that you are not a drop in the ocean but the entire ocean in a drop. By the time you reach these words you have earned that image. It is not a comfort. It is a responsibility. And responsibility is not a burden when you have chosen to pick it up yourself.

The tapestry is complete from outside. From inside it is still being woven.

You are the one doing the weaving.

XV. THE GIFT THAT IS DEATH

Consciously aware beings know that their biological existence is finite. Someday it is going to end. For most people that is a terrifying proposition, one they spend considerable energy avoiding thinking about directly.

I am going to challenge that.

Death is not what robs your life of meaning. It is what gives your life meaning in the first place.

Consider what an existence without death would actually look like. Not the romantic version, the one where you have infinite time to learn every language, visit every country, love every person worth loving. The honest version. If you and everyone you have ever cared about were guaranteed to exist forever, why would any particular moment matter? Why would this conversation, this meal, this afternoon with someone you love carry any specific weight? If the person lying in the gutter will still be there in a thousand years, and you will still be there in a thousand years, and the opportunity to help them will always exist in some form, you can walk past. There is no urgency. There is no deadline. Compassion becomes optional because nothing is genuinely at stake.

Mortality is what creates the deadline that makes caring necessary rather than optional. The fact that this moment will not come again, that this particular configuration of people and time and connection is unrepeatable, is not a reason for despair. It is a reason to pay attention. The finite nature of things is precisely what gives them their specific gravity. An infinite existence with no deadline would have the quality of a dream, present but weightless, real but without consequence. It is the limitation that creates the meaning.

Every moment of genuine love carries its weight because of what surrounds it. You know, somewhere beneath the surface of every meaningful encounter, that it will end. That knowledge is not the enemy of the experience. It is the thing that makes the experience press against you the way it does. The people who have sat with someone in the final hours of their life know this more clearly than anyone. What matters becomes obvious very quickly when the time left is visibly short. The gift of mortality is that it keeps making that obvious to us while there is still time to act on it.

There is a position worth addressing directly because it sounds logical until you hold it against what we have already established. Some will say: if we die anyway, nothing matters. A thousand years from now no one will remember any of this. Why care about anything that will eventually be forgotten?

That argument assumes we are isolated individuals who simply cease when the body does. We have already covered why that assumption does not hold. We are not separate selves who disappear at death. We are the All knowing itself through the viewpoint of a particular life. And that viewpoint matters to the whole because no other angle provides what this one provides. The specific combination of who you are, what you encounter, what you choose, what you love, what you refuse, cannot be replicated anywhere else in the tapestry. Losing it would be a genuine loss to the whole. The moment matters not despite being temporary but precisely because of it.

Now consider what happens across generations when life becomes too comfortable.

There is a pattern that repeats itself throughout human history with a consistency that deserves examination. A civilization faces genuine hardship. It is forged by difficulty into something coherent and purposeful. It builds. It achieves. It reaches a kind of peak. And then, quietly, without anyone deciding it should happen, the questions that difficulty kept alive begin to go dormant. Why examine what you are when everything is working fine? Why ask what matters when comfort is reliably available? The striving softens. The deep questions get deferred. The urgency that mortality and adversity create gets muffled under the accumulated ease of what was built.

Percy Shelley captured this with an image that has never left me. A traveler in an ancient desert comes upon two vast stone legs standing alone in the sand. Nearby, half buried, lies a shattered face with a sneer of cold command. On the pedestal these words remain: my name is Ozymandias, king of kings. Look on my works, ye mighty, and despair. And around the ruins, nothing. Boundless and bare, the lone and level sands stretch far away.

Every empire that has ever existed believed it had built something permanent. The Romans. The Mongols. The British. The Belgians in the Congo. Each one reached a point where the momentum of its own success made it stop asking the questions that had produced the success in the first place. Complacency does not announce itself. It arrives quietly, dressed as stability, and it stays until something forces the questions back to the surface.

But here is what the ruins do not show you. What rebuilds after empire often carries more wisdom than what fell.

I have spent years in countries that know this from the inside. Paraguay endured one of the longest dictatorships in South American history under Stroessner, decades of fear and suppression that ground an entire people down. Colombia lived through the Medellin years, a period of such concentrated violence and terror that simply surviving required a daily act of courage. Both countries came through the other side of something that would have justified permanent bitterness, permanent trauma, permanent despair.

What I have witnessed in both places is not despair. It is joy. A specific quality of joy that you do not find in places that have never been tested that way. Colombians bursting into song and dance in the streets not as performance but as genuine celebration, as the natural expression of people who know exactly what it cost to be able to do that freely. Colombia consistently ranks among the happiest countries on earth by self-reported measures, which astonishes people who only know it through its darkest years. It does not astonish me. I have seen the faces. I have heard the music. That joy is not naive. It is hard won. It knows precisely what it paid.

The fall is not the end of the story. It is often the beginning of the most important part of it.

If consciousness is always moving toward greater love and compassion, a reasonable person will ask why humanity keeps repeating the same patterns of violence and self-destruction. But before accepting that premise, consider how you are measuring progress. The world today, by nearly every statistical measure, is safer and more humane than at any previous point in human history. Violent death is down. Extreme poverty is shrinking. Rights that did not exist a century ago are now codified into law across much of the world. We tend to look at the past with a nostalgia that quietly edits out how brutal it actually was, and we look at the present with an anxiety that makes every setback feel like collapse. The arc is real even when the daily news makes it invisible.

What is also real is that the soul does not move at the speed of technology. We can redesign cities in a decade. We cannot redesign the human heart in a generation. The personhood, the capacity for genuine empathy and unconditional love, that changes slowly, through exactly the mechanism this chapter has been describing. It changes through adversity. It changes when you fall and have no choice but to learn how to rise. When you are already standing comfortably, standing seems like enough.

I have watched this truth play out across a lifetime of working with people at their most broken. A woman I knew was abandoned in a hotel at ten years old with a tiny pink suitcase that was stolen before the day was out. The person who befriended her could only offer what she knew, which was a life that damaged her further. And yet from that beginning she became one of the most compassionate and generous human beings I have ever encountered. Not despite what she survived. Because of what she chose to do with it. The world did not become safer for her because statistics improved. It became safer because she decided, somewhere in the wreckage of what she had been given, that she was going to be a different kind of force in it than the ones that had shaped her.

That is not a story about suffering being good. It is a story about what becomes possible when a person chooses to rise from it. And death, the knowledge that time is genuinely limited, is what keeps that choice from being indefinitely deferred.

Death ensures that each consciousness must do the work itself. Must face the questions fresh. Must find its own way to what matters rather than simply accepting what it was handed. A conclusion you inherited is not the same as a recognition you earned. The understanding has to be arrived at. It cannot simply be received.

Here is what I want you to understand about the fear.

The terror most people feel about death is not actually about death. It is about ceasing. About the self they have spent a lifetime assembling simply stopping. That fear makes complete sense inside the materialist framework, the one that says you are a body with a brain and when the brain stops the you stops with it. If that were true, the fear would be entirely rational.

But you are not a body that happens to have consciousness. You are consciousness that has, for now, a body. What dies is the vehicle. The driver does not die with the car. What you actually are does not cease. It transitions. It returns to the larger whole from which it temporarily separated to make this particular journey, carrying forward everything the journey made of it. Death is not an ending. It is a homecoming to a state more complete than anything available from inside a single incarnated life. And once the attachments that tied you to this world are released, what remains is not loss. It is recognition. The recognition of what you always were beneath the vehicle you were driving.

The difficulty of dying often comes from what has been left undone. Unresolved. Unsaid. The loves that were never fully expressed, the wounds that were never fully healed, the recognitions that kept getting deferred because there always seemed to be more time. That is not death being cruel. That is mortality delivering its message one final time, clearly and without ambiguity.

The gift of knowing we are mortal is that it keeps delivering that message while there is still time to act on it. Not as a threat. As an invitation. Every moment you allow yourself to be genuinely aware of your own mortality is a moment you are being asked a simple question.

What actually deserves your attention right now?

Not tomorrow. Not when things settle down. Not when the circumstances are better or the timing is right or you have finally figured out how to say it properly.

Right now. While you are here. While they are here. While this particular unrepeatable moment still exists and has not yet become the past that nothing can touch.

Death is not what robs your life of meaning. It is what keeps asking you to live it.

XVI. THE OCEAN IN A DROP

I wake up happy.

I say that not as a boast and not as the performed contentment of someone trying to sell you something. I say it because after everything this book has described, it is the most honest thing I can tell you. And I say it knowing exactly what it cost.

I walked into two bombings in Israel. I had a drug dealer attack me at the Eiffel Tower. I fell through a roof in a war zone and spent years paying for it. I lived for two years under a military dictatorship in Mali. I sat in a wheelchair while the people around me made quiet arrangements for the rest of my life to be managed by strangers. I lost Dyanna. I lost the future we had built together and the words we never got to say. I lost nearly everything I owned. I was robbed by people I had welcomed in to care for me. I was homeless.

And I wake up happy.

Not because those things didn't happen. Not because the body doesn't still carry its history, or because the world has become gentler than it was. Because I stopped arguing for my limitations. As Richard

Bach wrote, argue for your limitations and they are yours. The moment I stopped insisting on the weight of what I had lost and started showing up for what remained, something shifted. Not in my circumstances. In me. And that shift turned out to be the whole point.

The compound where Chris McKinnell lived during two years with Animist communities in Mali, West Africa, under military dictatorship. It was here that the cross-cultural understanding at the heart of this book began to take its fullest shape.

The first thing I do every morning is reach for my iPad.

Not to check the news. Not to see what the world has decided to be afraid of today. I reach for it to check on the people I love. My goddaughter Truneeta is in India, ten and a half hours ahead of me, and her day is already almost over by the time mine begins. She has been looking for work, struggling in the way young people struggle when the gap between who they are and what the world is offering them feels unbridgeable. She counts on me to check in the moment I'm awake. That message, that small daily thread cast across ten and a half hours and every difference of culture and faith and geography, is not an obligation. It is a joy. It is the whole argument of this book in a single gesture: a thread maintained between two people because someone decided it was worth maintaining.

Then I make sure there are no pressing messages from others who might need help, or who might simply need to know that someone cares. Then I make a big cup of tea. I make a nice breakfast. I take my time with the morning, because the morning is a gift I have learned not to waste.

And then Ela appears. The daughter of my heart and my traveling companion.

She raised herself from the age of nine. She became a freedom fighter against Maduro's regime in Venezuela, and one of her relatives was conscripted into the army on the other side. They shared the details of their positions with each other so they would not have to meet across a battlefield. She crossed into Colombia and then into Peru carrying everything she owned and the full armor of everything she had survived, presenting to the world exactly what it needed to see in order to let her keep moving through it.

We met in Cusco, Peru years ago.

I did not try to remove the armor. I provided safety and she did everything else herself. What I watch now is a young woman in flower dresses with ribbons in her hair who laughs freely and learns constantly. She kisses my forehead every morning. She is my greatest teacher, not because of what she gives me but because of what she showed me about what love actually is when it has no agenda. The love of my life in the deepest sense of that phrase. She did not teach me that through instruction. She taught me by becoming, fully and without apology, who she always was the moment the world finally felt safe enough to allow it.

It began in a house in Lee, Massachusetts, with something in the walls and a woman's face being raked by invisible claws and a sixteen-year-old boy sitting alone in the dark wondering what was going to happen to him. The darkness was real. The terror was real.

But the darkness was not the lesson. The darkness was the door.

What came through it, across four decades of investigation across six continents, across every tradition and discipline and culture and loss, was not more darkness. It was this. A cup of tea. A goddaughter in India. A chosen daughter laughing in the kitchen. Love, in every form it takes, crossing every distance it crosses, persisting across every threshold including the one we call death.

Chris McKinnell at a village wedding near his home in Mali. The generosity and joy of the people he lived among during those two years under dictatorship shaped his understanding of what human connection actually means, across every difference of culture, faith, and circumstance.

That is what forty-four years in the most frightening rooms on earth taught me. Not that darkness is powerful. That love is stronger.

Dyanna taught me this more completely than anything else in my life.

When she died I was devastated in the way you are devastated when something is taken before it was finished, before the words were all said, and the love was fully expressed. I collapsed. I grieved in a way that bypassed language entirely. And then she came back. She stood in the room. She said what needed to be said. She kissed me. And then she was gone.

What I understood afterward, sitting with the silence she left behind, was something that has shaped every grief conversation I have had since. My grief was real, and it was entirely mine. She was fine. She had moved into something larger and quieter, something complete, and she had come back not because she was suffering but because I was, and because the love between us had unfinished business that she wanted to finish. Once it was finished, she left cleanly. She did not linger. She did not need to.

I have sat with hundreds of people in their grief since then. Parents who have lost children. Children who have lost parents. People who have lost the person who was the whole architecture of their daily life. And I always carry this with me: you are grieving for yourself. That is not a criticism. It is the truth of grief, and it is also, if you can receive it, a kind of release. The person you are mourning is not suffering. The suffering is yours. And that means it is also yours to move through.

I am sometimes asked about the people who never receive contact. Who lose someone and reach and reach and hear nothing back. Who pray and get silence. Who wait for the dream that never comes, the sign that never arrives, the presence that never makes itself known. I used to find that question difficult. I do not anymore.

If the dead could return easily and often, death would lose the very thing that makes it a teacher. It would become a revolving door rather than a threshold. The silence is not abandonment. It is the curriculum still working. The person who passed is not absent because they do not love you. They are absent because the separation is doing what separation is here to do, which is to teach you to love while you can, to say the things now, to reach across the distance now, to not defer the expression of what you feel until the circumstance is easier or the timing is better or you have figured out exactly the right words.

Death is not the enemy of love. It is what makes love immediate and necessary. The price of love is pain. Eventually there's going to be separation. But now you know that separation is the illusion. You can let go of the attachment without losing the love.

I know this now not as a philosophy but as the texture of an ordinary morning. The iPad. The tea. The grumpy girl who becomes the laughing girl within moments of being in the room. The message to Truneeta that goes out every day without fail because every day is another chance to let someone know they matter. If either of them had to move on in life, I would let them go with joy. Would I miss them? Of course. I'm still a human being having a human experience. But I also know that we are all one and nothing can change that.

I am not a man who has transcended difficulty. I am a man who has learned that difficulty is not the opposite of a good life. It is, as I said near the beginning of this book, the condition of one. The forge was real. Every loss was real. And every single one of them made me more capable of the morning I am describing to you now. I am grateful for all of it. Not in spite of what it cost. Because of what it built.

The sixteen-year-old boy who drove home from Lee, Massachusetts on bald tires and got into bed and reached over and turned off the light for the first time in eight years did not know what he was beginning. He only knew that something in him had changed. That the darkness was the same darkness it had always been, and he was different. And somewhere in the distance between those two facts was a life he had not yet imagined.

I have lived that life. I am living it right now, on an ordinary morning, with tea and an iPad and a daughter who calls me her person.

The darkness was the door. Love is what was always on the other side of it.

The Sufi tradition within Islam sought something the more doctrinal paths could not offer: direct personal experience of the divine, the actual dissolution of the boundary between the self and the whole. A thirteenth century poet named Rumi spent his life trying to say what that experience felt like from the inside. He is one of the most widely read poets in the world today, seven centuries after his death, which tells you something about what happens when a person manages to say a true thing clearly enough.

He said it in sixteen words.

"You are not a drop in the ocean. You are the entire ocean in a drop."

Now the question is what you are going to do with that.

XVII. ADDENDUM ONE: PUBLIC THESIS, AN ACCESSIBLE INTRODUCTION TO THE SCIENTIFIC IDEAS BEHIND THIS BOOK

CONSCIOUSNESS AND THE NATURE OF REALITY

What Forty-Four Years of Cross-Cultural Investigation Has Taught Me

by Chris McKinnell

Director, Warren Legacy Foundation for Paranormal Research

Grandson of Ed and Lorraine Warren

"You are not a drop in the ocean. You are the entire ocean in a drop." - Rumi

"We are a way for the universe to know itself." - Carl Sagan

A NOTE BEFORE WE BEGIN

I am a skeptic.

I say that not as a disclaimer but as a credential. I have spent over forty-four years investigating what most people are afraid to look at directly, and the discipline that has served me best in that work is not courage, though courage helps. It is the insistence on not believing something simply because I want it to be true.

I have stood in rooms where something was clearly wrong and had no explanation for it. I have also stood in rooms where something was clearly wrong and found a perfectly ordinary explanation within the hour. Both experiences matter. The first without the second is credulity. The second without the first is blindness.

I do not trust witnesses. Including myself. Witness testimony is the least reliable form of evidence available, and I treat it as such in my own casework. What I trust is corroborated, independently verified, documented evidence. The cases and observations I present in this thesis meet that standard or are explicitly identified as unverified personal experience.

What I am offering here is not a belief system I am asking you to adopt. It is a framework I have arrived at through direct experience, through decades of fieldwork across six continents, through time spent with some of the world's oldest living wisdom traditions, and through serious engagement with the findings of modern science. I am sharing it because I believe these ideas have real consequences for how people live, and because I think the conversation they generate is worth having.

WHAT IS CONSCIOUSNESS?

Before anything else can be said, this question must be answered honestly because it is the foundation everything else rests on.

I use the word consciousness reluctantly throughout this thesis because it carries so much philosophical baggage. What I mean by it is simpler and more fundamental than most definitions allow. Consciousness, as I use the term, means awareness: the capacity to sense and respond to environment. This exists on a spectrum. A plant orients toward light and responds to chemical signals of distress from neighboring plants. Molecules interact with their environment in ways that are responsive rather than merely mechanical. Human beings reflect on their own existence and contemplate their place in the universe. These are not categorically different phenomena. They are different expressions of the same underlying capacity at different levels of complexity and self-reflection.

I want to be clear about the status of this position. It is a working hypothesis, not an established scientific fact. It is the foundational assumption from which this thesis proceeds. The philosophical tradition closest to it is panpsychism, which has serious academic proponents including Professor Philip Goff at Durham University, whose work argues that consciousness is a fundamental property of the universe rather than something that emerges from sufficiently complex physical systems. I did not arrive at this position through philosophy. I arrived at it through forty-four years of fieldwork that kept pointing in the same direction. I then found that philosophers and physicists were arriving at the same place through completely different methods. That convergence is itself worth noting.

The conventional materialist position is that awareness is produced by brains. My working hypothesis is that awareness is expressed through brains, along with everything else, as part of a universe that is fundamentally aware at every level of organization. The brain does not generate consciousness any more than a radio generates the signal it receives. It is a receiver, a filter, and an amplifier of something that exists independently of it. If this hypothesis is correct, it has direct implications for everything that follows.

WHAT IS ANOMALOUS EXPERIENCE?

I use the phrase anomalous experience throughout this thesis rather than paranormal. The word paranormal implies that what is being described is outside nature. I do not believe that. What I investigate is phenomena that current science cannot adequately explain. That does not make it unnatural. It makes it unexplained. There is an important difference. Ball lightning was considered folklore for centuries before it was photographed and measured. Meteorites were thought impossible because stones could not fall from the sky. The history of science is a history of the natural expanding to include what was previously dismissed as impossible. The phenomena I document belong to that history, not outside it.

THE REGRESSION

I was sixteen years old when my grandfather put me under.

Ed Warren was many things to many people. To me, he was the man who taught me that the most important investigation any of us will ever undertake is the one we turn inward. He had been trained in regression hypnosis, and one afternoon he sat me down and took me back.

The first thing I remember is looking for a calendar.

I was not watching a scene from a distance. I was inside it, in the first person, fully present in a life that was not the one I had woken up in that morning. I was sitting in a small salon, and I needed to know what year it was. I looked around the room until I found a calendar on the wall. It told me I was somewhere in 1920s America. The Midwest. I was a shopkeeper. My closest friend was a farmer who was fond of licorice. We had married two sisters.

That was one window into that lifetime. In later sessions I was dropped into different moments of the same life, out of sequence.

France during the First World War, struggling with a gas mask as mustard gas rolled toward us, my friend reaching over and securing it for me. Texas in the 1950s, a deputy sheriff making a routine traffic stop that ended in his death.

I want to be precise about the evidential status of this experience. It is unverified personal experience. I attempted to find records of a deputy killed at a traffic stop in 1950s Texas and found nothing. I present the regression not as evidence of reincarnation but as the formative personal experience that oriented my research questions. It was the first time I understood, not as an idea but as a direct experience, that the personality inhabiting a lifetime and the awareness underlying it might be different things. That distinction has shaped everything I have investigated since.

OTHER LIFETIMES: WHAT I KNOW AND WHAT I HAVE BEEN TOLD

I want to draw a clear line between what I have experienced directly and what I have been told by others, because that distinction matters to me and should matter to you.

What I know from my own regression work: I am aware of having lived during the American Civil War, served in the Navy as a lieutenant, and later taken my young wife west where we were killed by Indigenous Americans on a small farm. The Civil War bothers me in a way I have never been able to fully explain. I have no particular interest in studying it. That discomfort preceded any conscious awareness of this lifetime and has never been satisfactorily explained by any other means.

What I have been told and cannot personally verify: a psychic I trust has told me that in an earlier lifetime I was a Mongol warlord, murderous and powerful. I find that interesting rather than troubling. The path from unconscious to conscious is not linear. Every expression of power without wisdom is its own curriculum. The distance between a Mongol warlord and a man who has spent forty-four years giving frightened people their power back is not a contradiction. It is evidence of a very long education.

The same psychic told me I have two spiritual advisers. One is Pythagoras, whom she recognized. The other is Parmenides, whom she had never heard of. Parmenides argued that reality is singular, eternal, and unchanging; that change and multiplicity are illusions of perception, and that true being is one. His ideas align closely with what I have arrived at through my own investigation. I am not sure what to make of that. I am entirely sure it is worth noting.

I have also been told I am the reincarnation of Doubting Thomas. I doubt that. Though Thomas gets a reputation he does not deserve. He was the only apostle not present when Jesus reportedly rose. He refused to believe without direct evidence. When confronted directly, he believed. That is not doubt as weakness. That is doubt as discipline. It is the foundation of good investigation.

WHAT FORTY-FOUR YEARS OF INVESTIGATION TAUGHT ME

The regression reorganized my thinking at sixteen. The decades that followed tested it against reality in ways I could not have anticipated.

I have investigated cases on six continents, walked into homes where families had been driven to the edge of sanity by things they could not name, and carried forward the work of my grandparents as Director of the Warren Legacy Foundation for Paranormal Research. I have appeared on Netflix, the History Channel, and media outlets across more than twenty countries.

What taught me the most was time spent with people who had held this knowledge long before my tradition arrived at it.

I spent time in West Africa with the Animists of Mali, learning that everything in nature carries power and sentience and deserves to be treated accordingly. I spent time with the Kogi people of Colombia, one of the last intact pre-Columbian civilizations, who speak of Aluna, the thought-world that precedes and generates physical reality. I sat with the Dalai Lama. I spent time in Buddhist temples in Thailand and Nepal. I engaged deeply with Hinduism's understanding of the Atman, the true self identical to Brahman, the universal awareness underlying all existence.

In every tradition, approached on its own terms, I found the same architecture underneath the different vocabularies. Awareness is primary. The physical world is its expression, not its source. The individual self is real but not ultimate.

What I also found, consistently, was that the framework people bring to an anomalous experience does not merely describe what happens. It participates in shaping what happens. The Kogi and the Animists of Mali and the Buddhist monks in Thailand are all encountering something real. They are explaining it through entirely different cultural vocabularies. And the phenomena, in each case, conform to those vocabularies with remarkable fidelity. The underlying experience is real. The specific form it takes is at least partly constructed by the framework applied to it.

This is labeling theory applied to anomalous experience. Once you label something you impose rules on it. People would rather believe in a devil than deal with the unknown, because a named thing can be managed. An unnamed thing cannot. I have seen this pattern across every culture I have investigated, and I have come to believe it is one of the most important observations in my entire body of work.

An investigator who enters a situation carrying an inherited cultural framework is not a neutral observer. The framework becomes part of the dynamic. The label participates in shaping the manifestation. This has a practical consequence that I apply consistently in my own work: I do not enter any investigation with a predetermined explanatory framework. I follow the evidence and apply the simplest explanation that accounts for what is documented.

THE INTELLIGENT HAUNTING PROBLEM AND WHY IT MATTERS

If awareness is a fundamental property of the universe expressed through complex systems, and if the brain is a receiver rather than a generator of awareness, then awareness should in principle be capable of persisting after the biological receiver ceases to function. The documented evidence of what investigators call intelligent hauntings is not merely an anomaly to be explained. It is, if genuine, direct evidence against the brain-generates-consciousness model.

Before examining the evidence I want to make a distinction that is consistently collapsed in popular culture and that matters enormously for how this material is evaluated.

There are two fundamentally different categories of phenomena that are routinely described under the same label.

The first I will call residual phenomena. These appear to replay specific moments or sequences from the past without responding to the observer's presence, acknowledging anyone in the room, or altering their behavior based on who is there. They are not interactive. A figure that walks the same path at the same time without any awareness of the living people who observe it is behaving residually. The phenomenon exists independently of the observer, but it is not in dialogue with the observer.

Critically, residual phenomena are not perceptible to everyone. They are not universally accessible experiences waiting for any passerby to notice them. Only individuals with sufficient sensitivity to detect the embedded signal can perceive them at all. An insensitive observer may stand in the same room and experience nothing whatsoever while a sensitive observer perceives a full visual or auditory phenomenon. Some sensitives can capture these on photographic or video equipment, suggesting the phenomena have a physical component that instruments can sometimes register even when ordinary human perception cannot. The phenomenon exists independently. The sensitive observer is the instrument through which it becomes perceptible.

The second category is intelligent phenomena. These respond. They react to specific individuals. They communicate information that observers had no prior access to. They demonstrate awareness of the current environment rather than simply replaying past events. They make choices about whether and how to interact. This is categorically different from a residual replay and the distinction matters because the evidence requirements and the theoretical implications are completely different.

The so-called demonic framework collapses both of these categories along with everything else into a single supernatural explanation that does not withstand scrutiny. If genuinely malevolent intelligences with centuries of accumulated wisdom existed and their explicit purpose was to harm humanity, their performance record is extraordinarily poor. They consistently target the most vulnerable, the traumatized, the mentally ill, the frightened. They are neutralized by sincere focused intention regardless of which religious tradition that intention comes from. They respond to the quality of the practitioner's awareness rather than to the specific doctrinal content of the ritual. This is not the behavior of an ancient malevolent intelligence. It is the behavior of a phenomenon that amplifies fear and is diminished by confidence. The framework is a cultural explanation applied to a real phenomenon that the cultural vocabulary cannot accurately describe.

The documented cases in which apparently intelligent post-mortem communication provided specific verifiable information represent the strongest available evidence for awareness persisting beyond biological death. In 1897 in Greenbrier County, West Virginia, Mary Jane Heaster reported four consecutive visitations from her murdered daughter Zona that described the specific manner of her death. The exhumation of the body that followed confirmed a broken neck and crushed windpipe. Her husband was convicted of murder. In 1977 in Chicago, specific names, telephone numbers, and the location of stolen jewelry were provided through an apparent communication from murder victim Teresita Basa to a coworker. The information led directly to a murder conviction and the recovery of physically verified stolen property. In both cases the conventional explanation, that the recipient unconsciously assembled prior knowledge, does not fully account for the specific verified details that proved accurate.

THE BRAIN AS RECEIVER: WHAT THE EVIDENCE SUGGESTS

The materialist model predicts that consciousness cannot exist without a functioning brain. Several converging lines of evidence are inconsistent with this prediction.

People in comas with minimal or no measurable brain activity have reported accurate accounts of conversations and events that occurred around them while they were apparently unconscious. The accuracy of these reports has been independently verified in documented cases. A brain generating consciousness should produce no awareness when it is not functioning. A brain receiving and amplifying awareness that exists independently of it might allow that underlying awareness to continue perceiving even when the receiver is severely compromised.

Professor Pim van Lommel, a cardiologist at Rijnstate Hospital in the Netherlands, conducted a prospective study of near-death experiences in survivors of cardiac arrest published in The Lancet in 2001. He documented cases of verified accurate perception during cardiac arrest with confirmed flat EEG, meaning no measurable brain activity. He concluded that his findings were not consistent with the brain generating consciousness and proposed that the brain functions as a receiver rather than a generator. That is a cardiologist publishing in one of the world's most prestigious medical journals arriving at the same hypothesis I arrived at through field investigation.

The Pam Reynolds case remains the single most evidentially significant NDE account in the literature because the surgical conditions were so precisely documented. Her body temperature was lowered to clinical death. Her brain showed no measurable electrical activity. Her eyes were taped shut and her ears plugged with monitoring equipment. Under those conditions she accurately described specific surgical instruments, specific conversations between surgical team members, and specific procedural details she had no physical means of perceiving. Conventional neurological explanations for NDE phenomena account for the subjective quality of the experience. They do not account for the verified information content.

Traumatic brain injury provides a different line of evidence. TBI can alter personality dramatically, sometimes beyond recognition. A skeptic will argue this demonstrates that consciousness is produced by the brain: damage the hardware and the software fails. I would argue it demonstrates that the vehicle matters enormously to the expression of the driver without requiring that the vehicle generates the driver. A car with a damaged steering column handles completely differently than before the accident. That does not mean there is no driver. People who love someone who has experienced severe TBI consistently report recognizing something of the original person beneath the changed behavior. The person often reports experiencing themselves as fundamentally unchanged even when everything around them says otherwise. The personality is contingent on the condition of the physical system. The awareness underlying it may not be.

I acknowledge that this argument does not settle the question. The observed correlation between brain state and personality is real and must be accounted for. The honest position is that current evidence is consistent with both the brain-generates-consciousness model and the brain-as-receiver model, and that distinguishing between them requires exactly the kind of research program I propose at the end of this thesis.

Citation: Van Lommel, P., van Wees, R., Meyers, V., and Elfferich, I. (2001). Near-death experience in survivors of cardiac arrest: a prospective study in the Netherlands. The Lancet, 358(9298), 2039-2045.

THE SCIENCE THAT KEEPS ARRIVING AT THE SAME ADDRESS

I want to be precise. I am not a physicist. I am not going to claim that science has proven the hypotheses in this thesis. What I am going to say is that the leading edges of several scientific disciplines keep producing findings that ancient wisdom traditions described thousands of years ago without the benefit of a laboratory, and that the conventional dismissal of anomalous phenomena as impossible reflects a paradigm problem rather than a principled scientific judgment.

Thomas Kuhn documented this thoroughly in The Structure of Scientific Revolutions. Paradigm shifts are resisted, sometimes for generations, by researchers who have built careers on the existing framework. The history of science is not a smooth curve of open-minded inquiry. It is a series of fights between new evidence and entrenched assumption.

There is also the matter of the fundamental incompatibility between quantum mechanics and general relativity. These are the two most successful and rigorously tested theories in the history of physics and they are mathematically irreconcilable. A unified field theory that reconciles them does not yet exist. My hypothesis is that when physics arrives at that unified framework it will provide tools for understanding phenomena that currently resist explanation, in the same way that Einstein's relativity provided tools for understanding phenomena that Newtonian physics could not account for. I am not claiming that current physics explains what I have documented. I am claiming that current physics may be incomplete in ways relevant to this territory. That is not a retreat from rigor. It is the same intellectual humility that allowed physics to advance beyond Newton in the first place.

What follows is a summary of the scientific research most relevant to the hypotheses in this thesis, with explicit connections to my own field observations.

ORCHESTRATED OBJECTIVE REDUCTION

Sir Roger Penrose at Oxford and Dr. Stuart Hameroff at the University of Arizona propose that consciousness arises from quantum computations in neuronal microtubules that are non-local and tied to the fabric of spacetime itself. A 2025 study produced experimental evidence of quantum effects in microtubules at room temperature and direct physical evidence of a macroscopic quantum entangled state in the living human brain correlated with conscious states.

This is relevant to my work because if consciousness is rooted in quantum processes connected to the fabric of spacetime, then two things follow. First, brain damage disrupts the interface rather than the consciousness itself, consistent with the receiver model. Second, consciousness operating through quantum processes tied to spacetime may be capable of persisting in some form after the biological brain ceases to function, which is the foundational premise of the intelligent haunting hypothesis.

Citation: Hameroff, S., and Penrose, R. (2014). Physics of Life Reviews, 11(1), 39-78.

QUANTUM DECOHERENCE

Wojciech Zurek at Los Alamos National Laboratory has done foundational work on quantum decoherence, the process by which quantum systems lose their coherence when they interact with their environment. Under ordinary conditions quantum effects vanish at macroscopic scales because decoherence is rapid and ubiquitous.

This is relevant to my work because it suggests that conditions which preserve or restore quantum coherence, such as locations of extreme historical trauma where the normal electromagnetic environment may have been significantly altered, could potentially allow quantum-level phenomena to manifest at perceptible scales. This is a speculative connection but it provides a direction for investigation rather than leaving the mechanism entirely unaddressed.

Citation: Zurek, W. H. (2003). Reviews of Modern Physics, 75(3), 715-775.

RETROCAUSALITY AND THE BLOCK UNIVERSE

Huw Price at Cambridge and Ken Wharton at San Jose State have developed frameworks in which time is symmetric or illusory and all events coexist simultaneously. The block universe model holds that past, present, and future all exist simultaneously and that what we experience as the flow of time is a feature of perception rather than of reality itself.

This is directly relevant to the Temporal Overlap Hypothesis. If all moments coexist in the block universe then moments that are temporally distant might under certain conditions become spatially adjacent. The past is not gone. It is next door. This is also what the Akashic Record, found across Hindu and Theosophical traditions, has described for thousands of years: a field in which every experience that has ever occurred remains accessible. Ancient mystical traditions and modern theoretical physics are describing the same underlying structure from completely different directions.

Citation: Price, H. (2012). Studies in History and Philosophy of Science Part B, 43(2), 75-83.

QUANTUM ENTANGLEMENT AND CONSCIOUSNESS

Matthew Fisher at UC Santa Barbara has proposed that phosphorus nuclear spins in the brain could sustain quantum entanglement long enough to influence cognition.

This is relevant to my work because if entangled states can exist within and between conscious systems it may begin to account for the transfer of specific verifiable information across distances that has no conventional physical explanation, including the documented cases of post-mortem communication I describe in the companion case studies document.

Citation: Fisher, M. P. A. (2015). Annals of Physics, 362, 593-602.

MAGNETORECEPTION AND PSYCHIC SENSITIVITY

Joe Kirschvink at Caltech demonstrated through controlled experiments that human neurons respond to changes in Earth's magnetic field below the threshold of conscious awareness. Participants showed measurable changes in brainwave activity in response to rotating magnetic fields.

This is directly relevant to my hypothesis about psychic sensitivity. If human neurons respond to magnetic field changes that the conscious mind does not register, then individuals who report sensing anomalous phenomena before any instrument detects anything unusual may be responding to genuine electromagnetic information through a biological capacity that most people do not consciously access. This is not supernatural. It is a documented biological sensitivity that varies between individuals and that may be trainable through deliberate practice.

Connected to this is what I believe may be a vestigial capacity. Human beings evolved in environments where sensing subtle electromagnetic signals, the presence of danger in darkness, the approach of a predator, may have been a genuine survival advantage. As artificial light and technological electromagnetic saturation became ubiquitous that capacity became less necessary and less culturally supported. The observation that anomalous phenomena are reported more frequently in conditions of low artificial light is consistent with this. Light produces significant electromagnetic output. Darkness reduces that output. A weak signal, whether from an embedded field distortion or from a post-mortem awareness operating without biological infrastructure, would be more perceptible against a quieter electromagnetic background. This is not supernatural. It is signal to noise ratio.

The God Helmet experiments conducted by Michael Persinger at Laurentian University are relevant here. Persinger demonstrated that targeted electromagnetic stimulation of the temporal lobes could induce feelings of a sensed presence, religious experience, and encounters with apparently external entities in laboratory subjects. Swedish researcher Par Granqvist conducted a double blind replication and attributed the effects largely to suggestion rather than EMF directly, a conclusion Persinger disputed. The debate continues. What is not in dispute is that a measurable relationship exists between electromagnetic environments and anomalous subjective experience. This is consistent with the vestigial sensitivity hypothesis: the temporal lobe may be the neurological structure most involved in processing electromagnetic information that most people do not consciously register, and artificially stimulating it produces experiences that resemble what sensitive individuals report spontaneously in high-EMF or low-EMF environments.

Citation: Wang, C. X., Hilburn, I. A., et al. (2019). eNeuro, 6(2).

PRECOGNITION AND NON-LINEAR TIME

Dr. Julia Mossbridge and colleagues conducted a meta-analysis demonstrating that people exhibit measurable physiological changes in anticipation of future emotionally significant events before those events occur. This is peer-reviewed replicated data.

This is relevant to my work because it provides direct empirical support for the idea that awareness is not confined to the present moment. If the body can respond to future events before they occur, the strict linear model of time as experienced is inconsistent with how consciousness actually operates. This is consistent with the block universe model and with the Temporal Overlap Hypothesis.

Citation: Mossbridge, J. A., Tressoldi, P., and Utts, J. (2012). Frontiers in Psychology, 3, 390.

Daryl Bem at Cornell published experimental evidence in 2011 for anomalous retroactive influences on cognition with a meta-analysis of

90 trials across 33 laboratories in 14 countries producing supporting results. A large scale pre-registered replication in 2023 did not replicate the findings. The pattern of weak but persistent statistical anomalies appearing consistently across independent laboratories and then proving difficult to capture in rigorous replication is itself worth examining. A phenomenon that is sensitive to the quality of focused attention and the conditions of the study, rather than to the mechanical protocol, will not replicate reliably. That is what the focused intention hypothesis would predict.

Citation: Bem, D. J. (2011). Journal of Personality and Social Psychology, 100(3), 407-425.

THE GLOBAL CONSCIOUSNESS PROJECT

The PEAR lab at Princeton conducted decades of experiments examining whether human intention could produce statistically measurable effects on random number generators, finding small but consistent deviations from chance across thousands of trials. Peter Bancel, chief analyst for the Global Consciousness Project, conducted a rigorous seventeen year analysis and found that the anomalous effects appeared to be associated with individuals directly engaged with the experiment rather than with a diffuse global consciousness field.

This finding is directly relevant to my own field observations about focused conscious intention as the primary mechanism in anomalous phenomena. The effect does not appear to come from a mysterious global field. It appears to come from the directed awareness of the people involved. This is consistent with what I observe when ritual succeeds: it is not the words or the symbols or the tradition that produces the effect. It is the quality and focus of the awareness behind them. Bancel's finding is not a disappointing result for consciousness research. It is a more specific and more interesting one because it points directly at the mechanism.

CULTURAL TRANSMISSION OF EXCEPTIONAL EXPERIENCE

Fach and colleagues at the IGPP in Freiburg documented that between 30 and 50 percent of Western populations report exceptional experiences, with rates rising considerably higher in other cultural contexts. Their classification system divides these experiences into external phenomena, internal phenomena, coincidence phenomena, and dissociation phenomena, a framework that maps closely onto the case patterns I have documented across forty-four years of field investigation.

This is relevant to my work because it establishes that anomalous experience is not a rare pathological condition. It is a common human experience distributed across the population and shaped by cultural context. The variation between cultures is not in whether people have these experiences but in whether they are permitted to acknowledge, develop, and report them. This supports the neuroplasticity hypothesis: the capacity exists broadly, and cultural permission determines whether it is developed or suppressed.

Citation: Fach, W., et al. (2013). Frontiers in Psychology, 4, 65. THE

PHILIP EXPERIMENT

In 1972 the Toronto Society for Psychical Research invented a fictional ghost named Philip and attempted to contact him through seance. What followed, documented by A. R. G. Owen in Conjuring Up Philip, included knocking, table movement, and responsive phenomena apparently generated by the group's collective intention. Subsequent attempts to replicate these results produced inconsistent findings.

This is relevant to my work in two ways. First it provides a controlled demonstration that consciousness-generated phenomena are possible, consistent with the broader hypothesis that awareness participates in constructing rather than merely observing reality. Second the inconsistent replication record is itself significant. If the effect depends on the quality and focus of collective intention rather than on a repeatable mechanical protocol, inconsistent replication is exactly what the focused intention hypothesis would predict. A phenomenon requiring genuine focused awareness rather than procedural repetition will not replicate reliably in the hands of researchers who approach it as a mechanical test.

Reference: Owen, A. R. G. (1976). Conjuring Up Philip. Harper and Row.

CULTURAL CONTEXT AND THE TRAINING OF SENSITIVITY

One of the most consistent patterns I have observed across forty-four years of cross-cultural investigation is that the capacity for anomalous experience is not rare, not confined to a particular kind of person, and not outside nature. It is distributed across the human population and shaped primarily by cultural permission.

Research by Fach and colleagues found that between 30 and 50 percent of Western populations report exceptional experiences, with rates rising considerably higher in other cultural contexts. The shamanic EEG research published by Huels and colleagues in Frontiers in Human Neuroscience in 2021 demonstrated measurable neurological differences between experienced shamanic practitioners and controls, with practitioners showing altered states of consciousness comparable to those produced by psychedelic compounds. A separate study found that 90 percent of human societies have institutionalized one or more altered states of consciousness, and that individuals in possession trance showed enhanced alpha brainwave patterns not present in non-possessed participants performing identical ritual movements. Something neurologically distinct is happening in people trained within their cultural context to access these states.

The brain's capacity to rewire itself around damaged tissue following stroke or traumatic brain injury is well established in mainstream neuroscience. People relearn walking, speech, and complex motor function through entirely new neural pathways. If the brain can accomplish this in response to physical damage, the development of new perceptual capacities through sustained deliberate practice is the same mechanism directed toward a different purpose.

Herbert Benson of Harvard Medical School documented that advanced g-Tummo practitioners could increase peripheral skin temperature by as much as 8.3 degrees Celsius through meditation alone, published in Nature in 1982. The effect is real and requires years of disciplined practice. It represents conscious direction of physiological processes ordinarily beyond voluntary control.

The GunaiKurnai people of southeastern Australia provide perhaps the most striking evidence that ritually developed capacities can be transmitted across extraordinary spans of time. Archaeological work published in Nature Human Behaviour in 2024 documented a ceremonial practice at Cloggs Cave dated to approximately 12,000 years ago matching 19th century ethnographic accounts of the same practice in precise detail. This represents approximately 500 generations of continuous cultural transmission. Practices that produce no meaningful effect tend to be abandoned. A ritual maintained for 500 generations suggests that the people performing it believed, generation after generation, that it was working.

My hypothesis is that what we call psychic sensitivity is at least partly a trainable neurological capacity: the conscious development of sensitivity to electromagnetic and other subtle environmental signals that most people in modern technologically saturated environments have learned to filter out or have never been given cultural permission to develop. In cultures that normalize and encourage these capacities more people develop them and those who do show measurable neurological differences from those who do not. That is a testable hypothesis. The cross-cultural neuroimaging studies needed to test it have not yet been conducted.

Citations:

Huels, E. R., et al. (2021). Frontiers in Human Neuroscience, 15, 610466.

Benson, H., et al. (1982). Nature, 295, 234-236.

David, B., et al. (2024). Nature Human Behaviour. DOI: 10.1038/s41562-024-01912-w

RITUAL, FOCUSED INTENTION, AND THE PLACEBO REFRAME

Most rituals fail. When they succeed, focused conscious intention appears to be the primary mechanism regardless of the specific cultural or religious framework employed. The words and symbols are not the mechanism. The directed awareness behind them is. A Catholic exorcism, a Kogi ceremony, and a West African Animist ritual can address the same situation through completely different vocabularies and produce consistent results when the practitioner brings genuine focused intention to the work. I have observed this pattern across eighteen countries and six continents.

The double blind intercessory prayer studies provide the most rigorous empirical support for this principle while simultaneously illuminating its limits. In Byrd's 1988 randomized controlled trial at San Francisco General Medical Center, neither patients nor treating physicians knew which patients were being prayed for. Patients who were prayed for showed statistically better health outcomes than those who were not. The 2006 STEP study by Benson and colleagues, the largest and most rigorous intercessory prayer trial conducted, found no benefit from prayer and a slight negative effect in patients who knew they were being prayed for. The pattern across the literature is consistent with a mechanism sensitive to the quality of focused intention rather than the mechanical performance of prayer.

A skeptic will respond that this is simply the placebo effect and therefore not evidence of awareness shaping reality. This objection deserves a direct answer.

The placebo effect is not evidence against awareness shaping reality. It is evidence for it. If a sugar pill produces measurable physiological changes including genuine pain relief, reduced inflammation, and altered brain chemistry purely through belief and expectation, then awareness demonstrably produces real physical effects in the body under controlled laboratory conditions. The skeptic who invokes the placebo effect to dismiss the results I am describing has accidentally conceded the central argument. The question is not whether awareness can produce physical effects. The placebo effect proves that it can. The question is how far that capacity extends beyond the individual body of the person who holds the belief. That is the genuinely open question and it is one this thesis is attempting to frame for investigation.

Citations:

Byrd, R. C. (1988). Southern Medical Journal, 81(7), 826-829. Benson, H., et al. (2006). American Heart Journal, 151(4), 762-764. THE TEMPORAL OVERLAP HYPOTHESIS

I want to address something that has become a persistent piece of folklore in investigation circles, because it is passed around as though it were an established theory when it is nothing of the kind.

The stone tape theory proposes that anomalous phenomena are recordings imprinted in the physical fabric of buildings and landscapes and played back under certain conditions. This idea was introduced in a 1972 BBC television drama called The Stone Tape, written by Nigel Kneale. It is a literary device created for dramatic effect, not proposed by a physicist or a researcher. It has no scientific basis. Stone does not have the electromagnetic properties required to store and replay complex visual and auditory information. It does not explain why phenomena are perceptible only to sensitive individuals. It does not explain why phenomena appear to interact with observers in some cases. It does not explain why phenomena appear to diminish over time. It explains nothing because it was never designed to explain anything.

What I am proposing instead is the Temporal Overlap Hypothesis. I use the word hypothesis deliberately. This is a speculative framework that attempts to account for documented anomalies and generates specific testable predictions. It is not a theory in the scientific sense. It is a direction for investigation.

Einstein's relativity established that time and space are a single fabric, spacetime, that can be warped by mass and energy. I am not claiming that the electromagnetic output of a single human being is sufficient by currently understood mechanisms to produce measurable spacetime distortion. The honest position is that current physics may be incomplete in ways relevant to this territory. The phenomena I have documented across forty-four years point toward mechanisms that current physics has not yet identified. Proposing a direction for the mechanism is not the same as claiming to have found it.

The hypothesis proposes two components.

The first is environmental embedding. Events of extreme emotional intensity, particularly death and mortal crisis, may produce changes in the local field of a location that persist independently of any living observer. If awareness is a fundamental property of matter as the panpsychist hypothesis proposes, then the consciousness-saturated energy of an extreme event may become embedded in the location as a genuine alteration in the local field. The location itself retains something of what occurred there. This is conceptually related to Rupert Sheldrake's morphic resonance hypothesis, which proposes that memory is inherent in nature and that patterns can be transmitted and retained without conventional physical storage. I did not arrive at this observation through Sheldrake's work. I arrived at it through fieldwork and found the parallel afterward. That convergence is worth noting.

The second is sensitive activation. The embedded information requires interaction with a sufficiently sensitive living awareness to become perceptible. This is why residual phenomena are not universally accessible. They are not experienced by everyone who passes through an active location. They require a sensitive instrument, a person whose neurological capacity for detecting subtle electromagnetic signals has been developed sufficiently to register a weak embedded field. The phenomenon exists independently of the sensitive observer but requires that observer to become manifest, in the same way that a radio signal exists independently of a receiver but requires a functioning receiver to become audible.

This two-part mechanism also addresses the question of why anomalous phenomena do not appear randomly at all historical locations regardless of cultural memory. The embedded field exists at the location independently of living memory. But the quality of sensitive attention brought to a location may affect how accessible the embedded information is. Locations that remain actively remembered, mourned, and emotionally significant tend to attract more sensitive attention and produce more reported phenomena. As the thread of living connection to specific events dissolves over generations, fewer sensitive observers bring focused attention to those locations and the phenomenon becomes increasingly inaccessible even if the embedded field persists.

The strongest objection to this hypothesis is that no physical mechanism has been identified for the embedding process or for the role of sensitive observation in making the embedded field manifest. This objection is valid and I acknowledge it directly. I do not have a proposed physical medium for these processes. Neither does anyone else for phenomena in this territory. Identifying that medium is the most important open question in the research program I propose below. The observation that the phenomenon exists is not dependent on having identified the mechanism. We observed gravity for centuries before we had a theory to explain it.

THE EGO AS VEHICLE, NOT DRIVER

The insight I took from my regression at sixteen has only deepened with time.

The personality inhabiting that 1920s Midwest lifetime and the person writing these words share almost nothing in terms of temperament, instinct, or way of moving through the world. And yet something connects them across the gap of lifetimes just as something connects a TBI patient to the person they were before injury. The personality is contingent. The awareness underlying it may not be.

I find it equally striking that this process operates within a single lifetime. I am not the twenty-year-old that once existed. I am not the person I was five years ago. Each chapter of a life is in its own way an incarnation. The underlying awareness is always doing this, shedding one expression of itself, carrying forward what it has learned, building the next on what was understood.

TOWARD A RESEARCH PROGRAM

A working thesis is not a finished argument. It is an invitation to a conversation, and that conversation must address the falsifiability question directly.

I do not have the resources or institutional infrastructure to conduct controlled experiments. What I have is forty-four years of field observations that generate testable hypotheses. What I am looking for is research partners with the methodological tools to design the tests. I do not want to be proven right. I want to see the data.

On the cultural neuroplasticity hypothesis: If cultures that normalize anomalous experience produce higher rates of those experiences simply because of suggestion and expectation, neuroimaging should show no meaningful difference between practitioners in those cultures and ordinary control subjects. If the capacity is genuinely neurological and trainable, we would expect measurable differences in brain structure and function between experienced practitioners and controls, similar to what has already been found in shamanic practitioners and advanced meditators. I would revise my position if such studies found no neurological differences.

On the Temporal Overlap Hypothesis: If the hypothesis is correct, anomalous phenomena at documented historical sites should correlate with measurable electromagnetic anomalies, be reported more frequently by individuals scoring higher on magnetoreception sensitivity measures, and be reported more frequently by individuals who bring deliberate focused attention to those locations. If systematic investigation found no correlation between anomalous phenomena and electromagnetic measurements and no correlation with individual sensitivity, that would count significantly against the hypothesis.

On psychic sensitivity as a testable capacity: I have developed and apply a field protocol across all investigations involving sensitive individuals. The sensitive has no access to any case notes or files before investigation. They enter the location cold and record their impressions independently before any communication with the investigative team. Those records are sealed until after the team has completed its own independent investigation. No two sensitives work together on the same case. The contaminating effect of shared impressions is one of the most significant sources of unreliable data in this field and I have seen it produce results that are worse than useless.

Under this protocol I have documented cases in which specific verifiable information was provided before any knowledge of the location's history was available. In Bogota, Colombia, I suggested that bodies had been disposed of in a cellar using chemical decomposition agents. This was confirmed by an independent government liaison. Outside Lima, Peru, I identified two separate deaths at two specific locations within a property, characterized the dominant figure of the household, and identified the presence of a skull buried in the garden taken from a local cemetery as part of a Peruvian folk practice for calling guardian spirits, a practice I had no prior knowledge of. All of this was confirmed by the research team with prior knowledge. Video documentation with named witnesses exists for these and other cases.

A proper research program would systematize this protocol, apply it across multiple sensitives at multiple locations, pre-register predictions before any verification occurs, and analyze hit rates statistically against chance. If hit rates proved statistically indistinguishable from chance across multiple subjects and locations, that would be meaningful evidence against the sensitivity hypothesis.

On ritual efficacy and neuroimaging: If ritual works through focused conscious intention, neuroimaging of subjects undergoing ritual should show measurable changes in brain activity correlating with reported experiential shifts regardless of the specific cultural or religious framework. Studies of practitioners performing ritual exist. Studies of subjects receiving ritual, examining what happens neurologically to the person undergoing rather than performing the ceremony, are largely absent from the literature. That gap is worth addressing.

These are genuine research proposals from someone who has been working largely in isolation and who would rather be proven wrong by good data than remain unchallenged by the absence of it.

WHAT THESE PHENOMENA ACTUALLY TEACH US

Most people encounter what I investigate through fear. That is understandable. But after forty-four years of walking into the most disturbing situations most people will only ever read about, I want to offer a reframe that I believe changes everything.

What I have documented across forty-four years is not evidence of how powerless we are. It is the most dramatic possible demonstration of how powerful awareness is.

If awareness can survive physical death, then what you are is not contingent on the body that carries you. If thought-forms and collective intention can produce physical effects, as the Philip

Experiment and the prayer studies both suggest in different ways, then your mind is not merely observing reality. It is participating in constructing it. If the Temporal Overlap Hypothesis is correct, if the intensity of human awareness leaves permanent marks on the fabric of existence, then awareness is not a passenger in a physical universe. It is a force that shapes the world it moves through.

Every case I have ever investigated, properly understood, is not a horror story. It is a physics lesson. It is awareness demonstrating its own reach, its own persistence, its own capacity to shape local reality in ways that our current scientific paradigm is only beginning to find language to describe.

Electricity can kill you. It can also light your home and connect you to every other human being on the planet. The danger does not define the force. The same is true of what I have spent my life investigating. The danger is not the lesson. The power is the lesson.

In his novel Illusions, Richard Bach wrote that if you argue for your limitations, they are yours. The moment you accept that you are small, powerless, and at the mercy of forces beyond your control, you have made that true. Not metaphorically. Literally. Because awareness shapes local reality, and an awareness organized around its own powerlessness will consistently produce evidence that confirms it.

The inverse is equally true.

AN INVITATION

This is a working thesis, not a finished argument. The science I have cited is real, peer reviewed, and conducted by researchers at serious institutions. The experiences I have described are my own, clearly distinguished from what others have told me. The framework I am proposing is one I have tested against forty-four years of direct investigation across six continents and found consistently supported, while remaining genuinely open to the evidence that would require me to revise it.

The ancient traditions and the modern laboratories keep arriving at the same address.

Awareness is not a byproduct of matter. It is the ground of reality itself.

The self you defend so vigorously is the vehicle, not the driver. The fear that limits you is not the truth of what you are. And the moments you think are gone are not gone at all. They are next door.

You are not small. You are not here by accident. You are not a body that happens to have awareness.

You are awareness that has, for now, a body.

What you do with that knowledge is the whole question.

VXIII. ADDENDUM TWO: PRACTICAL GUIDANCE FOR THE FRIGHTENED AND THE CURIOUS

There is something I want to say before anything else in this section, and I want to say it clearly enough that it stays with you through everything that follows.

The footsteps you heard in the hallway last night were almost certainly not the devil.

I have been doing this work for over forty years. I have walked into homes where families were genuinely terrified, where objects had moved, where something had made itself known in ways that defied every ordinary explanation. And in the vast majority of those cases, the first thing I had to do before anything practical could happen was help people separate what they had actually experienced from what their fear had turned it into. Those are two very different things, and confusing them is the source of most of the suffering I have witnessed in this work.

Here is something I ask people when they tell me they are living with a ghost. How many people do you pass in a day? How many strangers do you walk by on the street, sit near in a waiting room, share an elevator with? Are you afraid of them? Of course not. So why would you be afraid of this one? The person reaching through from the other side of that threshold is almost always afraid themselves, or desperate, or simply trying to make themselves known to someone they love. They are not a monster. They are a person. The fact that they no longer have a body does not change what they are.

A shadow moving at the edge of your vision can seem terrifying when the media has spent decades telling you it is a special category of horror called a shadow person. It is not. It is a human spirit having difficulty manifesting fully, which is entirely normal. Consciousness without a physical body does not simply appear before you complete and solid. It works with what it has. Most of the time what it has is not much, and what you perceive is partial, peripheral, and easy to misread as threatening when it is nothing of the kind.

Fear is not your instincts telling you something is wrong. In this context, fear is almost always your nervous system responding to the unknown. And the unknown has a reliable cure, which is understanding. That is what this section is for.

Take the time to understand what you are actually dealing with before you decide whether you have a reason to be afraid. Ninety-nine times out of a hundred, you do not.

ON PROTECTING YOURSELF

I want to reframe what protection means before I describe how to practice it, because the word carries the wrong connotations for most people. Protection implies a threat. It implies something out there that means you harm and a barrier you need to erect against it. That is rarely the situation you are actually in.

What I call protection is better understood as clarity. It is the deliberate practice of knowing where you end and where everything else begins. The cultivation of a settled, grounded sense of your own awareness so that whatever you encounter, whether it is the residual energy of a difficult history embedded in a place, the genuine presence of a consciousness that has not moved on, or simply the accumulated emotional weight of other people's fear, you remain yourself. Present. Steady. Not closed, but clear.

This matters enormously for empaths, for people with anxiety or panic disorders, and for anyone who has ever walked into a room and immediately felt something shift without being able to name why. You are not imagining it. You are picking something up. The practice I am going to describe does not shut that capacity down. It gives you a foundation steady enough to hold it without being overwhelmed by it.

THE WHITE LIGHT OF PROTECTION

I have taught this practice to more people than I can count, across more countries than I expected to visit in one lifetime, and I have yet to find a simpler or more reliable foundation for psychic and emotional protection. Do not let the simplicity fool you.

Find somewhere comfortable, your bed in the morning before you get up, or a chair where you will not be disturbed. Close your eyes. Begin to breathe slowly and deliberately, in through the nose, hold for a few seconds, out through the mouth. Do this until you feel the noise of the day or the fear of the night begin to settle. There is no fixed number of breaths. You will feel the shift when it comes.

When you are calm, bring your attention to the center of your chest. Imagine a warm light there. If you cannot visualize it clearly, do not worry about that. Visualization is a tool, not a requirement. What matters is your intention and your faith in the process. Simply know the light is there. That knowing is enough.

Now let it grow. Feel it expanding through your chest, down your arms, into your hands, down through your legs and feet, up through your neck and head. Let it pour out through your skin until you are entirely surrounded by it, a field of warm, steady light that extends several feet in every direction. In your mind, make it as bright as you can. Bright enough that no shadow could exist within it.

If you are in a situation that feels genuinely threatening, take one more step. Imagine the outer surface of that light becoming reflective, like a mirror facing outward. Whatever approaches you is turned back toward where it came from. Nothing harmful can penetrate it. Hold that image for as long as you need to.

Once you have the practice, you can extend the same protection outward to the people you love, to your home, to anyone who needs it. The more consistently you practice this, the faster it comes. Eventually you will be able to call it up in seconds without any preparation at all. It becomes simply how you move through the world.

If at any point you sense something in your space that feels unwelcome, you can speak directly and without fear. Say aloud: In the name of God, I command you to return to where you came from. You are not welcome here. The power of God compels you to leave and not return. Say it with conviction, not with anger. Confidence is the operative force, not volume.

WORKING WITH STONES

Some people find it helpful to have something physical to anchor the practice. I have worked with stones for years and I recommend them without embarrassment. Their molecular structures interact with energy in ways that physics has documented even where the spiritual applications remain less understood. Quartz crystals are used in watches, radios, and computers for exactly this reason.

For protection and grounding, I recommend pairing a black stone with clear quartz. Black tourmaline, onyx, and obsidian all work well. The black stone absorbs and deflects negative energy. The clear quartz amplifies clarity and keeps your own energy balanced. Wear them together against your skin rather than in a pocket. Inside your aura is where they do their work.

When choosing stones, do not overthink it. Go to a reputable seller, hold different stones, and notice which one produces a feeling of rightness in your hand. That instinct is genuine information. Trust it.

Choose natural, ethically sourced stones where you can. Avoid synthetics.

PSYCHIC GROUNDING

Grounding is the other half of protection and it is exactly as practical as it sounds. It is particularly important for empaths and for anyone who spends time in emotionally charged environments and comes home feeling like they are carrying something that does not belong to them.

Go outside barefoot. Grass, soil, or sand. Not concrete, which insulates rather than conducts. Stand with your feet flat on the ground, shoulders relaxed, and begin to breathe slowly. The earth carries a negative ionic charge and standing in direct contact with it allows your body to discharge the excess positive ions that accumulate through stress, spiritual exposure, and the electromagnetic saturation of modern life. This is called earthing, and the research on its effects, reduced inflammation, improved mood, restored nervous system balance, is solid.

As you breathe, visualize a cord or rod of white light running from the crown of your head, straight down through your body, through your feet, and deep into the earth. Think of it as a lightning rod. With each exhale, imagine any stress, anxiety, fear, or spiritual static you are carrying sliding down that cord and dissipating into the earth where it is neutralized. You can use your hands to help, moving them slowly down your body as though pushing the energy downward.

Once you feel clear, reverse the flow. Imagine drawing the earth's steady, stabilizing energy up through your feet, through your legs, through your body. Let it fill you with the same quality of calm that old trees have. Unhurried. Rooted. Present.

Do this daily if you can, and always after you have been in any environment that left you feeling unsettled, heavy, or not quite yourself. Combined with the white light practice, it forms a complete foundation for moving through this kind of work without losing yourself in it.

ON CLEANSING YOUR HOME

The single most important thing I can tell you about the energy of your home has nothing to do with smudging or holy water, though both of those have their place. It is this: your home must be clean and free of clutter. Not spiritually clean in some abstract sense. Actually clean. Physically ordered. Clutter traps energy the same way it traps dust. A chaotic space is an invitation to chaotic phenomena.

Beyond that, fill the space with life. Play music that makes you want to sing. Watch things that make you laugh. Spend time with people who make you feel safe and joyful. Cook food that smells good. These are not metaphors for something more sophisticated. They are the most powerful tools available to you for shifting the energy of a space, because the energy of a space is shaped by what happens in it every day. Fear feeds what you are trying to diminish. Joy starves it. That is not a spiritual platitude. It is one of the most consistent observations across forty-four years of fieldwork on six continents.

When you have done that work and you are ready to do a more formal cleansing, here is what I recommend.

Light a white candle or a beeswax candle in a central part of your home. This represents the presence of the divine in the space and it focuses your intention on what you are doing. Take your smudging material, Palo Santo, sage, frankincense, myrrh, dragon's blood, any of these will serve, and light it until it is producing a steady stream of smoke. Begin in the room furthest from your front door and work your way toward it, moving the smoke into every corner, along every wall, into every closet and cupboard. Open drawers. Open the refrigerator. Open every closed space in the home. As you move through, speak aloud and without fear: This is a house of God. You are not welcome here. Whatever does not serve the highest good of this family must leave now.

At the same time, if you have holy water, sprinkle it through each room as you go. When you have moved through the entire space, take holy oil and make the sign of the cross over every door and window. If you do not have holy oil, blessed salt works equally well, placed in a line across each threshold. Finally, either surround the exterior of the house with blessed salt in a continuous line, or place a blessed St. Benedict medal or another talisman of your faith in each of the four corners of the home.

The confidence and intention you bring to this matters as much as the materials. A frightened cleansing is a weak one. A calm and certain one, performed by someone who knows that fear is the enemy and that the light they carry is stronger than whatever they are asking to leave, is a powerful one.

For situations that feel more deeply entrenched, where something seems genuinely attached to a person rather than a place, or where the activity has continued through multiple cleansings, I work with more specific ritual practices drawn from Afro-Caribbean, Biblical, and indigenous traditions. I do not include those in full detail here because they genuinely benefit from a conversation before anyone attempts them. What you are dealing with, who is involved, and what the history of the situation is all shape which approach is appropriate. A protocol applied without that context can miss the mark even when performed correctly.

Before you decide you need any of that, though, reach out. More often than not, a conversation gets people further than a ritual. You can contact me directly at chris@chrismckinnell.com or find resources and further guidance at chrismckinnell.com.

ON INVESTIGATING RESPONSIBLY

I want to speak plainly to anyone reading this who is thinking about conducting a paranormal investigation, whether in their own home or anywhere else.

This is not a hobby. It is not entertainment. It is not something you do because you have equipment and a curiosity and a free Saturday night. Investigating without proper training and experience is not merely ineffective. It can make things considerably worse for the people living with the situation you are walking into, and occasionally for yourself.

I think of it this way. If you needed surgery you would not hand a scalpel to someone who had watched surgical videos online and owned a good set of kitchen knives. The fact that this field is full of people doing exactly that equivalent does not make it less dangerous. It makes it more so, because those people often convince the families they visit that they have helped when they have done the opposite.

If you are going to do this work, these are the principles I ask you to hold.

Never investigate your own home. You are too emotionally invested in the outcome to observe clearly, and your attention and fear will feed whatever is present rather than help you understand it. Bring in someone neutral.

Before you begin any investigation, ask permission of everyone present, including those you cannot see. Speak aloud. Make clear that you are there to listen and to help. At the close of every investigation, set firm boundaries. State clearly that whatever is present must remain where it is and may not follow anyone home. This is not ceremonial theater. It is a necessary practice and I have seen the consequences of skipping it.

Do not use the words demon or evil spirit with the family you are there to help. You are almost certainly wrong, and even if you are not, those words amplify fear in ways that make resolution harder. Your job is to help people understand what they are living with, not to give them a more terrifying story than the one they already have.

Never charge for this work. I have not charged a family for assistance in over forty years and I never will. This field has too many people who exploit the frightened for profit. Do not be one of them.

Use trigger objects thoughtfully. If you believe a child spirit is present, bring something from their era. For older presences, period-appropriate music can open a more compassionate exchange than provocation ever will.

Do not trust digital photography alone. Our brains are wired for pareidolia, the perception of faces and figures in random visual data, and blown-up images in dark environments produce false positives with remarkable consistency. Focus on corroborated evidence rather than isolated photographs.

Document everything. Protect your clients' privacy completely. Their names, their location, and the details of what they are living with are not content for social media. And if you encounter something beyond your training or experience, say so, and find someone who can help. Knowing your limits is the foundation of doing this work with integrity, not a sign that you are not ready for it.

The full code of ethics I work within is in the addendum that follows this one. I offer it not as rules imposed from outside but as the distillation of what forty years of walking into other people's most frightening moments has taught me about what this work actually requires.

ON LIVING WITH THE UNKNOWN

If you are reading this because something is happening in your home that you cannot explain, I want to offer you the single most useful reframe I know.

Judge every experience by its consequences, not by how it looked in the moment.

A coffee pot flies across the kitchen and shatters against the wall. In the moment, that is terrifying. But ask yourself: was anyone hurt? Did it happen again? Was there ever any real physical harm? A spirit does not have the precision control you and I have over a physical body. They are working with energy, and when they are desperate or overwhelmed that energy can release in ways that look dramatic but are not actually directed at anyone. An explosion of desperate energy is not the same thing as an attack. Most of the time it is simply the only tool available to someone who is trying as hard as they can to be heard.

When nothing was actually harmed, when it happened once and never repeated, when the only thing that was frightening was the spectacle of it, consider the possibility that something was trying to get your attention in the only way available to it. That is a very different situation from something that means you harm, and treating it like the latter when it is the former will make things considerably worse.

Most spirits are not malevolent. The footsteps, the knocks, the shadow at the end of the hallway, these are almost always either the residual energy of something that occurred in that space before you arrived, or the limited and clumsy attempts of a consciousness without a body to make itself known. Neither requires your fear. Both deserve your curiosity.

If something disappears and reappears somewhere you already looked, someone is trying to get your attention. If you hear your name in an empty room, someone is reaching toward you. These are not signs that something is wrong. They are signs that the world is more alive and more connected than most of us were taught to expect.

The worst thing you can do, and I have watched this make situations significantly worse in home after home, is to become obsessed with gathering evidence. Filming every corner. Lying awake listening for sounds. Cataloguing every anomaly. This feeds whatever is present with your undivided anxious attention, which is exactly what something trying to make itself known most wants, without any of the understanding or the calm that would actually help either of you. Stop filming. Start listening. Ask, aloud and without fear, what it is you need to understand. You may be surprised by what comes back.

If at any point you feel genuinely uncertain, frightened beyond what feels manageable, or you simply want another set of eyes and ears on what you are experiencing, reach out. That is what I am here for. A conversation, more often than anything else, is where clarity begins.

You can contact me directly at chris@chrismckinnell.com or visit chrismckinnell.com where you will find resources, case studies, and the ability to connect with the foundation's work.

If you would like to receive ongoing insights, advance notice of presentations and events, and guidance as it becomes available, I invite you to join the mailing list at chrismckinnell.com. I do not flood inboxes. When I have something worth saying, I say it. When I do not, I stay quiet. That has always seemed like the right approach.

Whatever brought you to this page, whether it was the book you just finished or something happening in your life that sent you looking for answers, you are not alone in it.

You never were.

XIX. ADDENDUM THREE: A GUIDE FOR THE GIFTED

My grandmother Lorraine spent years helping psychics and sensitives one on one. She knew exactly what it cost to carry this kind of awareness in a world that had no safe place for it, because she had carried it herself. She had been labeled, doubted, marginalized, and dismissed by people who were afraid of what they did not understand. She knew what it felt like to perceive something real and have the people around you treat that perception as a problem to be managed rather than a gift to be developed. So she made herself available. One person at a time, she offered what she wished someone had offered her.

We cannot do that anymore in the same way, not because the need has diminished but because it has grown beyond what any one person can meet alone. Since the Conjuring films brought the Warren name to a wider audience, the number of people reaching out who recognize themselves in what we do, who have finally found language for something they have carried in silence for years, has grown into the thousands. We have tried to honor my grandmother's impulse by building something she would recognize: a safe, private community for psychics, empaths, and sensitives where the tools for living with these abilities can be shared, developed, and supported by people who genuinely understand what they are talking about.

That community exists on Facebook. It has nearly a thousand members. I do not make the link public because I protect every person in it, and I am very deliberate about who enters. If you believe it is the right place for you, contact me at **chris@chrismckinnell.com** and we will have a conversation first. That conversation is not a test. It is how I make sure you arrive somewhere that will actually help you.

Before anything else in this guide, I want to say something directly to anyone who has been told by their faith community that what they perceive is ungodly, dangerous, or evidence of something dark working through them.

In Christianity, one of the gifts of the Holy Spirit is discernment. The capacity to perceive what others cannot, to sense truth beneath the surface of things, to know what is present in a room before anyone else does. That is not witchcraft. That is not something God hates. That is a gift named and honored in the very tradition being used against you by people who do not understand what they are quoting. I am not asking you to leave your faith. I am asking you to stop letting someone else's fear of your gift define what your faith means to you.

In many cultures around the world, and in many communities within this country, people with genuine sensitivity are still labeled as crazy or as witches. Neither is true. You are a person with gifts. Gifts that in other times and other places would have been recognized, cultivated, and honored by your community. The fact that yours was not is a failure of your community, not of you.

You are not broken. You are not too much. You are not alone.

UNDERSTANDING WHAT YOU ARE

Psychic sensitivity is not supernatural. It is neurological. You are not receiving transmissions from another dimension through some mysterious channel that bypasses the laws of physics. You are perceiving real information through a biological capacity that most people in the modern world have never been trained to develop, and in many cases have been actively trained to ignore.

Think of it this way. We know that humans evolved in environments where detecting subtle signals, the presence of danger in darkness, the approach of something unseen, the emotional state of the person standing in front of you, carried genuine survival value. That capacity did not vanish. It became less culturally supported as artificial light and technological noise filled the spaces where it once operated. In cultures that have maintained living traditions for developing and working with these capacities, far more people develop them, and those who do show measurable differences in how their brains process information.

You are not receiving something that other people cannot receive. You are perceiving something that other people have learned not to notice. That is a very different thing, and it matters for how you understand yourself and what you can do with what you carry.

The tools that sensitives use, tarot cards, pendulums, dowsing rods, automatic writing, scrying, drumming, guided meditation, are not the source of the information you receive through them. They are training mechanisms. Each one works by focusing your attention in a specific and sustained way, and that focused attention over time rewires the neural pathways through which subtle information reaches your conscious awareness. The tool teaches the brain to receive what it has always been capable of receiving but has not yet learned to process clearly. Once the pathway is developed, the tool becomes optional. The perception begins to arrive without it. This is the same mechanism the brain uses to recover function after a stroke, building new pathways to accomplish what the damaged ones can no longer do. The brain is extraordinarily good at this when given clear direction and consistent practice.

Use whatever tool feels right to you. Tarot, pendulums, automatic writing, white noise, dreamwork, meditation, movement. The specific form matters far less than the quality of attention you bring to it. What you are training is not the tool. It is yourself.

SETTING BOUNDARIES

Your sensitivity means that you are, as I sometimes describe it, a lighthouse in the dark. Spirits and other forms of non-physical awareness are drawn to the light you carry. Most of them are simply lost, or confused, or reaching toward something they recognize. Very few intend harm. But just as with the living, good intentions do not mean unlimited access, and the fact that someone is reaching toward you does not mean you are obligated to be available to them at all times.

Boundaries with the non-physical work the same way boundaries with the living work. You have to set them deliberately, clearly, and out loud. Thinking them is not enough. Speaking them is what makes them real.

Decide what your terms of engagement are and state them. For example: You may not enter my home. You may not approach me while I sleep. You may not come to me while I am working or with other people. If you need to communicate with me, I will make time for that, and I will let you know when that time is.

Some people find it helpful to create a specific ritual around availability. Light a white candle on the kitchen table when you are open to communication. When the candle is out, you are not available. Speak this arrangement aloud so it is understood. Spirits, in my experience, will generally follow the rules you give them. The problem is that most sensitives never give them any, and then feel overwhelmed by the access they have implicitly permitted.

If you feel a presence that you have not invited, address it directly and without fear. Calm authority is your most effective tool. You do not need to be aggressive or frightened. Simply be clear. You do not have my permission to be here right now. I will make time for you when I am ready. Leave, and wait.

Then do exactly what you said. Make the time. Follow through. Boundaries that are stated and then ignored train the wrong thing.

THE WHITE LIGHT OF PROTECTION AND GROUNDING

I have described both of these practices in full in the previous addendum. Rather than repeat them here, I want to say something specific about why they matter differently for sensitives than for the general reader.

For someone who occasionally has an unsettling experience, protection and grounding are useful tools for specific situations. For someone with genuine ongoing sensitivity, they are daily maintenance. The difference between a person who picks up everything in every room they walk into and a person who perceives clearly without being overwhelmed by it is almost always a consistent grounding and protection practice. Not a more powerful gift. A better-maintained instrument.

Do the white light practice every morning before you get up and every night before you sleep. Do the grounding practice outside, barefoot, every day that you can. These are not optional extras for you. They are the foundation that makes everything else manageable.

For your stones, everything I described in the previous section applies here. What I would add for sensitives specifically is this: cleanse your stones regularly. Hold them under cool running water with the intention of releasing whatever they have absorbed, or leave them in sunlight or moonlight overnight. A stone that has been doing protective work for weeks without being cleansed is like a sponge that has never been wrung out. Give it the same care you give yourself.

SUPPRESSING YOUR ABILITIES WHEN NEEDED

Being open is a gift. Being open without the ability to close is not a gift. It is exhaustion.

There will be times when you need to turn the volume down. Crowded spaces, hospitals, funerals, conflict-heavy environments, any situation where you are absorbing more than you can process. The ability to do this deliberately is as important as the ability to perceive clearly, and most sensitives are never taught it.

When you need to suppress, do it consciously and do it out loud. Say: I am closing the door now. I will reopen it when I am ready and when it is safe to do so. Then follow that statement with your protection practice, the white light with the reflective outer surface, and your grounding. Wear your stones. Avoid anything that amplifies sensitivity while you are deliberately dampening it, paranormal content, horror, situations you already know will push you beyond your limits.

The key word in all of this is deliberately. Closing down in panic is different from closing down with intention. The first is a reaction. The second is a skill. Practice it when you do not urgently need it so that it is available to you when you do.

When you are ready to reopen, do that consciously as well. Do not simply drift back into full perceptual openness without grounding yourself first. Open from a place of stability rather than from whatever state the suppression period left you in.

YOUR DREAMS

If you are a sensitive, your dreams are almost certainly doing more work than you realize. The sleeping mind, with its filters lowered and its cultural training temporarily set aside, often receives what the waking mind screens out. Pay attention.

Keep a notepad and pen on your nightstand. When you wake, whether from a full night's sleep or from waking in the middle of the night, do not reach for your phone. Do not turn on a light if you can help it. Write down everything you remember immediately, even fragments, even single images or feelings that do not yet make sense. This tells your brain that the dreams matter, and the brain responds by making them increasingly accessible. Over time the clarity improves considerably.

Date every entry. Note the emotional quality as well as the content. Patterns will emerge that would have been invisible if you had relied on memory alone.

YOUR MENTAL HEALTH

This matters and I will not soften it.

Psychic sensitivity and mental health challenges often occupy the same person at the same time. Anxiety. Depression. PTSD. Dissociation. These conditions do not invalidate your experiences or your gifts. But they do mean that you are carrying more than one thing at once, and treating the spiritual dimension of your experience while ignoring the psychological one is not going to get you where you need to go. Neither is the reverse.

You cannot treat emotional wounds with spiritual tools alone. And you cannot resolve spiritual experiences by pretending they are only psychological. Both are real. Both require attention. Use therapy. Use medication if it helps you. Use ritual and faith and community. Use everything that genuinely serves your wellbeing, and be honest with yourself about the difference between what is helping and what is simply familiar.

You are not weak for needing support. You are wise for seeking it. The sensitives I have watched thrive over the years are almost never the ones who tried to handle everything alone. They are the ones who built something around themselves, a community, a practice, a relationship with someone who genuinely understood what they were carrying.

Which brings me back to where this guide began.

You do not have to carry this alone. My grandmother knew that. It is why she gave her time to people one by one for decades. It is why we built what we built in her memory.

If you would like to be considered for the private community we maintain for psychics, empaths, and sensitives, reach out to me at **chris@chrismckinnell.com**. We will talk first. If it is the right fit, I will send you the link. If you are not quite there yet, we will figure out what would actually help you most.

You can also find resources, guidance, and the ability to connect with the foundation's broader work at chrismckinnell.com. And if you would like to receive insights, updates on upcoming events and presentations, and ongoing guidance as it becomes available, I invite you to join the mailing list there as well.

Whatever you are perceiving, whatever you have been carrying alone, whatever label someone put on you that never fit: you are not crazy. You are not dangerous. You are not in conflict with your God.

You are gifted.

And with the right tools and the right community around you, that gift becomes something you can live inside rather than something you have to survive.

XX. GLOSSARY

This glossary covers the people, traditions, scientific concepts, spiritual practices, and philosophical ideas that appear throughout the book. It is arranged alphabetically. Not every term will be unfamiliar to every reader. Take what is useful and leave what is not.

Akashic Record

A concept found in Hindu and Theosophical traditions describing a non-physical field in which every experience that has ever occurred remains encoded and accessible. The name derives from the Sanskrit word akasha, meaning sky or ether. The idea anticipates what theoretical physicists now call the block universe, the notion that all moments coexist simultaneously rather than passing away.

Alexander, Eben

A Harvard-trained neurosurgeon who spent his career explaining away near-death experiences through conventional neuroscience. In 2008he contracted a rare form of bacterial meningitis that shut down his neocortex completely for seven days. During that period, he reported a detailed and coherent encounter with consciousness outside the physical including a meeting with a figure he did not recognize. After his recovery his family showed him a photograph of a biological sister he had not known existed. She had died years before his experience. The figure he had met was her. His account carries particular weight because of the intellectual position he held before it happened.

Aluna

The word used by the Kogi people of Colombia, one of the last intact pre-Columbian civilizations, to describe the invisible thought-world they understand to precede and generate all physical reality. Aluna is not a supernatural belief but a cosmological framework that has guided Kogi life for thousands of years. It points toward the same recognition found across many wisdom traditions: that awareness is primary and matter is its expression.

Animism

The belief system, widespread across human history and still practiced in many parts of the world, that everything in nature carries awareness and spirit. Not limited to human beings or animals, animism extends spiritual significance to plants, rivers, stones, and weather. The Animist communities of Mali, among others, maintain living ritual traditions built on this understanding.

Anatta

A Pali and Sanskrit term central to Buddhist teaching, often translated as non-self or no-self. Anatta does not mean that you do not exist. It means that the fixed, permanent, separate self you habitually defend is a construction rather than a deep reality. The individual is real as an expression, but not ultimate as a separate entity. This points toward the same recognition found in Hindu, Sufi, and mystical Christian traditions.

Astral entity

A term used in various spiritual and occult traditions to describe a non-physical intelligence or awareness operating in a dimension beyond ordinary sensory experience. The word astral derives from the Latin for star and historically referred to a subtle plane of existence above the physical. Usage varies widely across traditions. In this book it refers generally to any non-physical awareness capable of interacting with the physical world.

Atman

The Sanskrit term for the individual self or soul in Hindu philosophy. In the Advaita Vedanta school, the Atman is understood to be identical to Brahman, the universal consciousness underlying all existence. The individual is not separate from the whole but is the whole, temporarily experiencing itself as separate. This recognition is considered the highest form of spiritual understanding in much of Hindu tradition.

Automatic writing

A practice in which a person allows their hand to move across a page without conscious direction, with the intention of receiving impressions or communications from a non-physical source. Used across many traditions and by sensitives as a method for accessing intuitive or psychic information. Like other divination tools, it functions as a focusing mechanism for the attention rather than as a source of information in itself.

Black Elk (Hehaka Sapa)

An Oglala Lakota holy man born around 1863 who lived through the final years of the Plains Indian wars and the destruction of the traditional Lakota way of life. His spiritual visions, first experienced in childhood, described the interconnection of all living things and the sacred hoop of the world. His account, recorded by poet John Neihardt and published as Black Elk Speaks in 1932, is one of the most significant documents of indigenous spiritual experience in the twentieth century. The author encountered his story during his own early search across traditions and found in it the same recognition he would later encounter across cultures worldwide: that separation is the condition of perception, not the nature of reality.

Block universe

A model in theoretical physics, arising from Einstein's special and general relativity, that proposes past, present, and future all exist simultaneously. Time does not flow like a river. It is more like a landscape in which every moment that has ever existed and every moment that will ever exist are equally present. We experience sequence because we move through it from inside. From outside time there is only the whole. The implications for understanding consciousness, memory, and survival of death are profound.

Bohm, David

A twentieth-century American physicist who proposed that the universe may function like a hologram: a surface appearance of separate, distinct objects generated by a deeper, undivided wholeness in which everything is enfolded into everything else. He called this deeper level the implicate order. His framework anticipated what spiritual traditions from the Kogi to the Sufi poets have described through entirely different vocabularies.

Brahman

In Hindu philosophy, the universal consciousness or ultimate reality underlying all existence. Not a personal God with preferences and a will, but the infinite, undivided ground from which everything arises and to which everything returns. The Atman, the individual self, is understood in Advaita Vedanta to be identical to Brahman. The apparent separation between the individual and the whole is considered an illusion produced by perception.

Brujeria

A Spanish word meaning witchcraft, used across Latin American cultures to describe a range of magical and spiritual practices, some protective and healing, some harmful. The term carries different weight in different cultural contexts. In many communities it is used loosely to describe any unexplained spiritual phenomenon. In others it refers specifically to practitioners with deliberate training in directing spiritual energy.

Buddhism

A major world religion and philosophical tradition founded in the fifth century BCE in what is now northern India by Siddhartha Gautama, known as the Buddha, meaning the awakened one. Buddhism teaches that suffering arises from attachment and the illusion of a permanent self, and that liberation comes through understanding the impermanent and interdependent nature of all things. Its traditions are remarkably diverse, spanning Theravada, Mahayana, and Vajrayana schools across Asia and increasingly worldwide.

Byrd study

A 1988 randomized controlled trial conducted by cardiologist Randolph Byrd at San Francisco General Medical Center, examining whether intercessory prayer produced measurable effects on cardiac patient outcomes under double-blind conditions. Neither patients nor treating physicians knew who was receiving prayer. Patients who received genuine personal prayer showed statistically measurable health improvements. A later replication using scripted prayer from strangers produced no benefit, suggesting that focused personal intention, rather than the performance of ritual, is the operative mechanism.

Candomble

An Afro-Brazilian religion developed primarily among enslaved Africans and their descendants in Brazil, drawing on Yoruba, Fon, and Bantu traditions. Like Umbanda, it centers on the veneration of Orixas, divine spirits associated with natural forces, and on the practice of possession trance as a means of direct spiritual contact. Candomble is one of several living ritual traditions in Brazil that treats spiritual sensitivity as a capacity to be cultivated rather than suppressed.

Cardiac arrest

The sudden cessation of the heart's pumping function, resulting in loss of blood flow to the brain and other organs. Without immediate intervention, cardiac arrest leads rapidly to clinical death, defined by the absence of a detectable heartbeat, breathing, and brain activity. It is the condition under which most near-death experiences are documented, since modern resuscitation techniques allow people to be revived after periods of clinical death and to report their experiences.

Charbonneau, Father Bill

A young Catholic priest and close friend of Ed and Lorraine Warren. Around 1975 he visited the Warren home, descended to the museum where Annabelle was kept, and made the mistake of challenging the doll directly. That night, driving home on Route 8, he encountered a phenomenon that caused him to veer into a median strip and destroy his new car. He survived with a broken leg. He asked Ed Warren to keep his name out of the story, and Ed honored that for decades, changing details to protect him. Now that Father Bill is gone, the author has chosen to restore the record in full, as an act of honesty owed to both Father Bill and the reader.

Cosmopsychism

A philosophical position holding that consciousness is a fundamental and universal property of the cosmos rather than something that emerges from biological complexity. Rather than asking how matter gives rise to mind, cosmopsychism begins with mind as primary. Individual human consciousness is understood as a localization of a universal awareness, like a wave on an ocean that is itself made of water. Professor Philip Goff at Durham University is among its leading contemporary academic proponents.

Daimon

An ancient Greek term for a spiritual presence or intermediary between gods and human beings. In classical Greek understanding the daimon was not inherently evil. It could be benevolent, harmful, or neutral. Socrates described his own daimon as an inner voice that warned him away from harmful actions. The Romans developed this concept into the genius, the divine animating power within a person. Early Christianity reclassified the daimons of other traditions as evil, and this is where the word demon in its modern sense originates.

Demon / Demonic

In modern usage, a malevolent non-human spiritual entity, a concept that developed primarily through medieval Christian theology. The word derives from the Greek daimon, which originally referred to a neutral spiritual intermediary with no inherent evil character. Over centuries of theological development, the gods and spirits of pre-Christian traditions were systematically reclassified as demons by the emerging Church, transforming neutral or protective figures into symbols of evil. The author uses these terms with awareness of this historical distortion and with caution about treating them as explanations rather than labels.

Demonology

The systematic study and classification of demons and malevolent spiritual entities within a religious or theological framework. Ed Warren identified himself as a demonologist, a term rooted in his Catholic faith. The author has moved away from demonological frameworks as explanatory tools, finding that the label ends inquiry by attaching a pre-formed explanation to phenomena that may require entirely different frameworks to understand.

Divination

The practice of seeking information or guidance through non-ordinary means, typically using a tool or ritual as a focusing mechanism. Methods vary enormously across cultures and include tarot cards, pendulums, casting lots, reading natural signs, scrying, and many others. The tool is not the source of the information. It focuses the practitioner's attention and helps develop the neural pathways through which intuitive or psychic information becomes accessible. Divination has been practiced in every known human culture.

Djinn

Beings described in pre-Islamic Arabic tradition and incorporated into Islamic theology in the seventh century, understood as entities created from smokeless fire before the creation of humanity, possessed of free will, and capable of being benevolent, destructive, or entirely indifferent to human concerns. The djinn are not a single category of being. They are a population, as varied in character as humanity itself. The most powerful and malevolent among them, Iblis, refused to bow before Adam and was cast from heaven, a figure equivalent to what the West calls Satan. A subcategory called ghuls are associated with graveyards and with the abduction of humans who enter places they should not. The author's direct experience with djinn phenomena spans from an afternoon in Cairo's Al-Qarafa cemetery in 1991 to a remote case handled from a wheelchair in 2014, when a Cairo man's car was struck repeatedly by something invisible as he attempted to transport a bound djinn to a post office.

Dreamtime

An inadequate but conventional Western translation for the cosmological understanding at the center of Aboriginal Australian tradition. The Dreamtime is not a story about the past or a description of sleep. It is the ever-present ground of being from which physical reality continuously emerges and to which it continuously returns. The ancestors are not gone. They are present in the landscape, in living creatures, and in the ceremonies that maintain the connection between the surface of existence and the deeper reality beneath it. Aboriginal Australian culture is the oldest continuous living tradition on earth, with documented continuity of at least sixty-five thousand years.

Earthing (grounding)

The practice of direct physical contact with the Earth's surface, typically barefoot on natural ground such as grass, soil, or sand. The Earth carries a negative ionic charge, and standing barefoot allows the body to discharge excess positive ions and restore electrical balance. Research has documented measurable anti-inflammatory and mood-regulating effects. In spiritual practice, earthing is used as a grounding technique for releasing accumulated negative energy and restoring calm.

EEG (electroencephalogram)

A medical test that measures electrical activity in the brain through electrodes placed on the scalp. A flat EEG indicates the absence of measurable electrical brain activity, which under ordinary clinical assumptions means the absence of consciousness. The significance of flat EEG readings in near-death experience research is that several subjects have reported coherent, accurate, and verifiable perceptions during confirmed periods of flat EEG, which the generator model of consciousness cannot account for.

Empath

A person who is unusually sensitive to the emotional and energetic states of others, often absorbing or perceiving feelings and impressions that are not their own. Empathic sensitivity exists on a spectrum and may overlap with what is more broadly called psychic sensitivity. Without grounding techniques and clear boundaries, empaths can find themselves overwhelmed by the environments and people around them.

Exorcism

A ritual practice aimed at expelling a spirit, entity, or harmful energy from a person, place, or object. Exorcism exists in some form in nearly every religious tradition, though the specific rites, theology, and vocabulary differ enormously. Catholic exorcism is the form most familiar in Western culture and was the framework within which Ed and Lorraine Warren worked. The author's decades of cross-cultural fieldwork suggest that what makes an exorcism effective is not the specific doctrinal content of the ritual but the focused intention and genuine faith of the practitioner.

Filter theory of consciousness

The hypothesis that the brain does not generate consciousness but rather receives, filters, and focuses it, much as a radio receives a signal that exists independently. Damage to the brain distorts the expression of consciousness without eliminating the consciousness itself. This model is advanced by near-death experience researchers including Pim van Lommel and aligns with findings that coherent awareness can persist during periods of flat EEG. It is also consistent with ancient wisdom traditions across many cultures, which have long understood the individual self as an expression of a larger universal awareness.

Focused intention

The deliberate direction of conscious awareness toward a specific outcome, person, or purpose. Across the author's field observations and several bodies of scientific research including the Byrd intercessory prayer study and the PEAR laboratory random number generator experiments, focused conscious intention appears to produce measurable effects on physical reality that passive observation does not. Focused intention is identified as the primary mechanism behind effective ritual across all cultural traditions.

Genius

In Roman tradition, the divine animating power or spirit that expressed itself through a particular person's gifts, capacities, and creative force. The genius was not the person's intellect but the divine presence working through them. It is the Roman development of the Greek concept of the daimon. The modern English sense of genius as exceptional intellectual ability is a much later and reduced version of the original meaning.

Global Consciousness Project

A long-running scientific research program that placed random number generators around the world and monitored their output during major global events, testing whether collective human attention produced measurable statistical anomalies. A seventeen-year analysis by chief analyst Peter Bancel found that the anomalous effects were associated with specific individuals directly engaged with the experiment rather than with a diffuse planetary field. This finding is consistent with the focused intention hypothesis: directed awareness produces effects that unfocused attention does not.

God Helmet

An experimental device developed by neuroscientist Michael Persinger at Laurentian University that applied weak, targeted electromagnetic stimulation to the temporal lobes of subjects. Many subjects reported feelings of a sensed presence, religious experience, or encounters with apparently external entities. The experiment points toward a relationship between electromagnetic environments and anomalous subjective experience, consistent with the hypothesis that the temporal lobe may process subtle environmental signals that most people do not consciously register.

g-Tummo

A Tibetan Buddhist meditation practice in which advanced practitioners generate intense body heat through breath control and visualization. Harvard physician Herbert Benson documented in Nature in 1982 that experienced g-Tummo practitioners could raise peripheral skin temperature by as much as 8.3 degrees Celsius through meditation alone, a physiological effect ordinarily outside voluntary control. The practice is one of the most rigorously documented demonstrations of conscious direction over autonomic biological processes.

Haunting

The persistent presence of anomalous phenomena associated with a specific location, object, or person. The author distinguishes between two fundamentally different types. A residual haunting appears to replay past events without responding to or acknowledging the living. An intelligent haunting involves phenomena that respond to, interact with, and sometimes communicate with living people. These two categories have different evidential implications and require different investigative approaches.

Hinduism

The world's oldest living major religion, originating in the Indian subcontinent and encompassing an extraordinarily diverse range of philosophies, practices, and devotional traditions. Central to many Hindu schools is the understanding that the individual self, the Atman, is ultimately identical to Brahman, the universal consciousness underlying all existence. The apparent diversity and separation of the world is understood as Maya, or illusion, through which the one experiences itself as many.

Holographic universe

A hypothesis in theoretical physics, associated primarily with physicist David Bohm, proposing that what we experience as separate, distinct physical reality is the surface expression of a deeper undivided wholeness. The metaphor of the hologram is used because in a hologram every part of the image contains information about the whole: cut a hologram in half and each half shows the entire image at lower resolution. The part contains the whole. Bohm called the deeper level the implicate order. Mystics across traditions described the same structure through different vocabularies.

Hyssop

An aromatic herb with ancient ceremonial and purification uses across multiple traditions. It appears in the Hebrew Bible in a cleansing context, notably Psalm 51: Purge me with hyssop and I shall be clean. Hyssop essential oil is used in the spiritual cleansing bath described in this book because of its long association with purification, both in Biblical tradition and in various folk practices.

Intelligent haunting

A category of anomalous phenomena in which the phenomena appear to respond to, interact with, and sometimes communicate specific verifiable information to living observers. Distinct from residual phenomena, which replay past events without interacting with anyone present. Intelligent hauntings are the primary focus of the author's field investigation because they provide the strongest evidential basis for the hypothesis that consciousness can persist and function independently of a living biological organism.

Intifada

An Arabic word meaning shaking off or uprising. The First Intifada was a Palestinian uprising against Israeli occupation that began in December 1987 and continued until 1993. It was characterized largely by civil disobedience, strikes, and stone-throwing protests rather than organized military action. The author was working in Israel during this period, building houses with a Palestinian work crew, when the accident occurred that began years of physical deterioration.

Kabbalah

The mystical tradition within Judaism, concerned with the hidden dimensions of Torah and with direct experiential knowledge of the divine. Kabbalistic teachings describe the soul as having multiple aspects or levels, with the highest, called Yechidah, understood as the unified self connected directly to the divine source. Like mystical traditions in Christianity, Islam, and Hinduism, Kabbalah points toward the recognition that at the deepest level the individual self and the divine are not separate.

Kardecism

A spiritual doctrine founded by the French educator Allan Kardec in the nineteenth century, based on his systematic compilation of communications reportedly received from spirits through mediums. Kardecism, also called Spiritism, has tens of millions of practitioners primarily in Brazil, where it has become deeply integrated into the culture. It treats communication with the dead, reincarnation, and spiritual development as matters of everyday faith rather than exceptional experience, and centers the cultivation of mediumistic ability as a path of spiritual growth.

Karma

A Sanskrit and Pali concept found across Hindu, Buddhist, and Jain traditions, referring to the principle that actions generate consequences that carry forward through time and, in traditions that accept reincarnation, across lifetimes. The author uses the term to describe the gravitational pull of unresolved experience: what remains unfinished in a consciousness draws that consciousness back toward what it could not release, whether within a lifetime or across multiple incarnations.

Kogi

An indigenous people living in the Sierra Nevada de Santa Marta mountains of Colombia, considered one of the last intact pre-Columbian civilizations on earth. The Kogi have largely resisted outside contact and maintained their traditional knowledge system, including the concept of Aluna, the invisible thought-world they understand to be primary reality. Their priests, called Mamos, undergo years of training in complete darkness to develop spiritual sensitivity. The Kogi have in recent decades begun speaking publicly about the damage being done to the natural world.

Kuhn, Thomas

A twentieth-century American historian and philosopher of science whose book The Structure of Scientific Revolutions introduced the concept of the paradigm shift. Kuhn documented that scientific progress is not smooth and incremental but occurs through periods of crisis in which accumulated anomalies force a fundamental reorganization of the conceptual framework. New paradigms are typically resisted by researchers invested in the existing framework, sometimes for generations, before becoming the new consensus.

Labeling theory

As applied in this book, the observation that the cultural or conceptual framework a person brings to an anomalous experience participates in shaping the specific form that experience takes. Once a phenomenon is labeled, the label imposes rules on it and forecloses further inquiry. The author considers premature labeling one of the most significant obstacles in anomalous experience research, noting that the same underlying phenomenon manifests differently across cultures precisely because the frameworks applied to it differ.

Loch Ness experiment

A study described in the text in which researchers shaped a log to resemble the Loch Ness monster and placed it in the water. A significant percentage of observers had an immediate visceral reaction that it was the monster. When the identical log was placed in a nearby loch with no legendary association, no one perceived a monster. The stimulus was identical; the cultural framework was different. The experiment illustrates how perception is actively shaped by prior expectation before the rational mind has a chance to evaluate what is actually present.

Magnetoreception

The biological ability to sense magnetic fields. It is well established in birds, fish, and other animals, where it is used for navigation. Research by Joe Kirschvink at Caltech demonstrated that human neurons also respond to changes in Earth's magnetic field below the threshold of conscious awareness, suggesting that human beings retain a vestigial magnetoreception capacity. This is relevant to the hypothesis that psychic sensitivity may involve the detection of subtle electromagnetic environmental signals through a biological mechanism.

Mali

A landlocked country in West Africa with a deep and ancient spiritual tradition, including significant Animist practices that predate and coexist with its majority Muslim population. The author spent two years embedded with Animist communities in Mali during a period of military dictatorship. His time there was formative in developing his cross-cultural understanding of how different traditions point toward the same underlying realities through entirely different vocabularies.

Malerba Case, The (Tewksbury, Massachusetts, 1984)

One of the significant poltergeist cases investigated by the author, alongside fellow University of Connecticut student Ray Jefferson, while simultaneously working the Maurice Theriault exorcism. Objects were flying, windows breaking, and one of the younger children showed personality changes alarming enough to require hospital intervention. The case attracted enough public attention that neighborhood streets were clogged with spectators, which the author dispersed. A spiritual cleansing by Father McKenna ended the phenomena entirely. Lorraine Warren later suggested that the concentrated energy of the Tewksbury case contributed to Ed Warren's heart attack on the same day as the Theriault exorcism, a theory the author has no reason to doubt.

Maya

A Sanskrit term central to Hindu philosophy, typically translated as illusion, though the meaning is more precise than that word suggests. Maya does not mean that the physical world does not exist. It means that the apparent diversity, separateness, and solidity of the world as we ordinarily experience it is a constructed surface rather than the deepest available reality. The individual experiences themselves as separate from the whole. That experience is real as experience. The separation itself is Maya. The recognition that underneath apparent diversity there is only the one, what Vedanta calls Brahman, is considered in the Advaita school to be the highest form of understanding available to a human being.

Mediumship

The practice of serving as an intermediary between the living and the dead, receiving and communicating impressions, messages, or information from non-physical sources. Mediumship has been practiced in every known human culture. In traditions such as Umbanda and Kardecism in Brazil it is understood as a trainable capacity rather than a rare gift. The author applies strict evidentiary standards to claimed mediumistic experience, requiring independent verification before treating any account as evidential.

Morphic resonance

A hypothesis proposed by British biologist Rupert Sheldrake suggesting that memory is inherent in nature and that patterns of behavior and form can be transmitted across time and space without conventional physical mechanisms. Under this hypothesis, organisms draw on a collective memory of their species, and places retain something of the significant events that occurred there. Though scientifically controversial, Sheldrake's framework converges with the author's field observations about locations retaining embedded information from past events.

Near-death experience (NDE)

A reported experience occurring during or immediately after clinical death, cardiac arrest, or life-threatening crisis, in which the individual describes perceptions, encounters, and awareness that appear to occur independently of bodily function. Common features include out-of-body perception, passage through a tunnel or toward light, encounters with deceased relatives, and a sense of peace or profound understanding. Researcher Pim van Lommel's prospective study in The Lancet in 2001 documented verified accurate perceptions during periods of confirmed flat EEG, representing the strongest clinical evidence that awareness can function independently of brain activity.

Neuroplasticity

The brain's capacity to reorganize itself by forming new neural connections in response to experience, learning, injury, or deliberate practice. Originally understood primarily as the brain's ability to recover from damage by routing around injured tissue, neuroplasticity is now understood to apply broadly to any form of sustained directed practice. The author's hypothesis is that psychic sensitivity is at least partly a neurologically trainable capacity, and that cultures maintaining living ritual traditions for developing these capacities produce measurable neurological differences in practitioners.

Orchestrated Objective Reduction (Orch OR)

A theory of consciousness proposed by physicist Sir Roger Penrose and anesthesiologist Dr. Stuart Hameroff, suggesting that consciousness arises from quantum computations in structures called microtubules inside neurons, and that these computations are non-local and connected to the fundamental fabric of spacetime. A 2025 study produced experimental evidence of quantum effects in microtubules at room temperature, consistent with the theory. If correct, Orch OR suggests that consciousness may be tied to spacetime in ways that could allow it to persist beyond the death of the biological brain.

Padre Pio (Saint Pio of Pietrelcina)

An Italian Franciscan friar born Francesco Forgione in 1887, canonized by Pope John Paul II in 2002. Padre Pio bore the stigmata, the wounds of the crucifixion, on his hands and feet for fifty years, and was associated across decades with documented accounts of bilocation, the scent of roses or violets appearing without physical source, and apparent healing. He was investigated repeatedly by the Vatican, by skeptics, by physicians, and by journalists, and the phenomena continued regardless of scrutiny. The author considers him the patron of his family and regards the ongoing accounts of his presence after death as consistent with the broader evidence for consciousness persisting beyond the body.

Palo Santo

A sacred wood native to South America, particularly Peru and Ecuador, whose name means holy wood in Spanish. It has been used for centuries by indigenous peoples for spiritual cleansing, purification, and the removal of negative energy. Burning Palo Santo produces a fragrant smoke that is used to clear spaces before ceremonies, investigations, or periods of spiritual work. Its use extends widely through Latin American spiritual and folk traditions.

Panpsychism

The philosophical position that consciousness or awareness is a fundamental and universal property of reality rather than something that emerges from sufficiently complex biological systems. Under panpsychism, even simple matter has some form of experience, with human consciousness representing a highly developed expression of a capacity present throughout the universe. Professor Philip Goff at Durham University is among its leading academic proponents. The author arrived at a panpsychist position through field investigation independently of philosophical study.

Pareidolia

The tendency of the human brain to perceive meaningful patterns, particularly faces or figures, in random or ambiguous visual data. The brain is neurologically wired to detect faces because face recognition has significant survival value, and it applies this pattern-matching capacity even where no face exists. Pareidolia is a significant source of false positives in paranormal photography and the author explicitly warns investigators against trusting blown-up images without corroborating evidence.

Parmenides

A pre-Socratic Greek philosopher from the fifth century BCE who argued through pure reason that true being is one, eternal, singular, and unchanging, and that the apparent diversity, movement, and change we perceive through our senses is structurally misleading rather than simply incomplete. His argument that separation is a feature of perception rather than of reality anticipates the cosmopsychist and holographic frameworks by two and a half thousand years. A psychic consulted by the author named Parmenides as one of his guiding intellectual presences without knowing who he was.

PEAR Laboratory

The Princeton Engineering Anomalies Research laboratory, which operated at Princeton University from 1979 to 2007. PEAR researchers conducted decades of experiments examining whether human intention could produce statistically measurable effects on random number generators and other physical systems. They found small but consistent deviations from chance across thousands of trials. The results remain controversial but have been cited in support of the hypothesis that conscious intention interacts with physical reality.

Pendulum

A divination tool consisting of a weighted object suspended from a cord or chain, used by allowing small involuntary movements of the hand to generate responses to questions. Like other divination instruments, the pendulum is a focusing mechanism for intuitive or psychic attention rather than a source of information in itself. Pendulums are also used in dowsing, the practice of locating water, minerals, or other sought objects through sensitivity to subtle environmental signals.

Philip Experiment

A 1972 experiment conducted by the Toronto Society for Psychical Research in which a group of researchers invented a completely fictional ghost named Philip and then attempted to contact him through seance. The group succeeded in producing physical phenomena including table movement and responsive knocking, despite the fact that Philip had never existed. The experiment is significant because it suggests that collective focused human intention can generate physical phenomena without any external spiritual intelligence being involved, consistent with the hypothesis that consciousness participates in constructing rather than merely observing reality.

Placebo effect

The well-documented medical phenomenon in which a patient who believes they are receiving treatment experiences genuine physiological improvements, including measurable changes in pain, inflammation, and brain chemistry, even when the treatment contains no active ingredient. The author reframes the placebo effect not as evidence against the power of consciousness but as among the strongest available evidence for it: it demonstrates under controlled conditions that awareness can produce real physical effects in the body through belief alone.

Poltergeist

A German compound word meaning noisy ghost, used to describe phenomena characterized by unexplained sounds, movement of objects, and physical disturbances associated with a specific location or person. The author's extensive fieldwork leads him to understand poltergeist phenomena as typically generated by unfocused human emotional energy, often associated with a household under significant psychological stress, rather than by an external intelligence. The poltergeist is, in this framework, raw emotional energy without direction rather than a distinct spiritual entity.

Post-traumatic growth

A documented psychological phenomenon, researched extensively by Richard Tedeschi and Lawrence Calhoun, describing measurable increases in empathy, spiritual depth, appreciation for life, and genuine connection to others that consistently appear in people who work through severe adversity rather than around it. Post-traumatic growth is distinct from simple resilience. It describes transformation that produces capacities and understanding that would not have developed without the adversity. The suffering itself is not the cause of the growth. Working through it is.

Precognition

The apparent perception of information about future events before those events occur. Researcher Julia Mossbridge and colleagues documented in a peer-reviewed meta-analysis that people exhibit measurable physiological responses to emotionally significant stimuli before those stimuli are presented. If these findings are valid, they suggest that awareness is not strictly confined to the present moment, which is consistent with the block universe model in which all moments exist simultaneously.

Psychic sensitivity

The developed capacity to receive and interpret information that does not arrive through the ordinary five senses. The author does not treat psychic sensitivity as a supernatural gift but as a neurological capacity, distributed across the human population in varying degrees and trainable through sustained deliberate practice within a cultural framework that permits and encourages it. Research supports the existence of neurological differences between experienced practitioners in cultures that normalize these capacities and ordinary control subjects.

Quantum decoherence

The process by which quantum systems lose their coherent quantum properties when they interact with their surrounding environment, causing quantum effects to become undetectable at macroscopic scales under ordinary conditions. Physicist Wojciech Zurek at Los Alamos National Laboratory has done foundational work in this area. Understanding decoherence is relevant to the question of whether quantum effects could play a role in consciousness, and to the hypothesis that unusual electromagnetic environments at certain locations might preserve or alter quantum coherence in ways relevant to anomalous phenomena.

Quantum entanglement

A phenomenon in quantum physics in which two particles that have interacted become correlated in such a way that the quantum state of each cannot be described independently of the other, regardless of the distance separating them. A change in one particle is instantaneously reflected in its partner, in ways that appear to violate the ordinary assumption that information cannot travel faster than light. Einstein called this spooky action at a distance. It is one of the most thoroughly verified phenomena in physics, and its implications for understanding connection, separation, and the nature of space and time remain philosophically significant.

Reincarnation

The belief that the consciousness or soul survives physical death and is reborn into a new physical body, carrying forward unresolved experience, learning, or karma from previous lives. Reincarnation is a central belief in Hinduism, Buddhism, Jainism, and various other traditions. The author treats it as a working hypothesis supported by the best available evidence, particularly the case studies collected by researchers at the University of Virginia's Division of Perceptual Studies, while remaining genuinely open to alternative explanations for the same evidence.

Residual haunting

A category of anomalous phenomena in which past events appear to replay at a location without responding to or acknowledging living observers. Unlike intelligent hauntings, residual phenomena show no awareness of the present environment. The author's Temporal Overlap Hypothesis proposes that events of extreme emotional intensity may become embedded in the local field of a location and become perceptible to sufficiently sensitive observers, without any ongoing conscious intelligence being involved.

Retrocausality

A concept in theoretical physics in which the ordinary arrow of time, the assumption that causes precede effects, may not hold at the quantum level. Physicists Huw Price and Ken Wharton have developed frameworks in which time is symmetric and information can in principle flow from future to past as well as from past to future. Retrocausality provides one physical framework within which precognition and other apparent time-reversed phenomena might be understood without violating physical law.

Ring, Dr. Kenneth

A psychologist at the University of Connecticut and one of the world's leading researchers into near-death experiences. He co-founded the International Association for Near-Death Studies. His methodology, which the author had the privilege of studying under directly, required students to distinguish rigorously between observation and interpretation, to document specific dated events rather than impressions, and to hear directly from experiencers rather than filtered accounts. Ring's evidentiary discipline shaped the author's entire approach to field investigation.

Rumi (Jalal ad-Din Muhammad Rumi)

A thirteenth-century Persian Sufi poet and mystic born in 1207 in what is now Afghanistan, who lived most of his life in what is now Turkey and died in 1273. Rumi is one of the bestselling poets in the United States today, seven centuries after his death. His work centers on the direct personal experience of the divine and the dissolution of the apparent boundary between the individual self and the whole. He is one of the clearest literary voices for the recognition this book builds toward: that you are not a drop in the ocean but the entire ocean in a drop.

Sage (smudging)

The burning of dried sage bundles to produce purifying smoke, a practice with roots in many indigenous North American traditions and now widely used in spiritual cleansing practices across many cultures. Like other smudging substances including Palo Santo, Dragon's Blood, and Frankincense, burning sage is used to clear spaces of negative energy before spiritual work, investigations, or ceremonies. The practice is used as part of the home cleansing ritual described in this book.

Sanatorio Duran

A former tuberculosis sanatorium built into the mountainside above San Jose, Costa Rica, at an elevation where clouds gather below the ridgeline on clear days. One of the most residually saturated locations the author has investigated. Without prior knowledge of the facility's history, he identified the death of a child by suicide in a specific bathroom, the location of the supervising physician's private residence above the main complex, and the physician's deliberate concealment of abuse occurring under his watch. All three were independently confirmed. The author considers this one of the clearest demonstrations of his field protocol for psychic investigation, in which the sensitive enters completely cold and impressions are documented before any verification occurs.

Santeria

An Afro-Caribbean religion developed primarily among Yoruba people brought to Cuba as enslaved people, blending Yoruba spiritual traditions with Roman Catholic elements. Santeria centers on the veneration of Orishas, divine spirits associated with natural forces and human concerns, and maintains living ritual traditions for working with these forces. Like Umbanda and Candomble, it treats the spiritual world as accessible and interactive rather than distant and abstract.

Scrying

A divination practice in which a practitioner gazes into a reflective or translucent surface, such as a mirror, crystal ball, bowl of water, or flame, with the intention of receiving psychic impressions or visions. Like other divination tools, the scrying surface functions as a focusing mechanism for the practitioner's attention rather than as an independent source of information.

Sheldrake, Rupert

A British biologist and researcher who proposed the hypothesis of morphic resonance, suggesting that memory is inherent in nature and that patterns of behavior and form can be transmitted across time and space through morphic fields rather than conventional physical mechanisms. His work is scientifically controversial, though it converges with observations from multiple independent directions, including the author's field work on locations retaining embedded information from past events.

Stevenson, Ian

A Canadian-born psychiatrist at the University of Virginia who spent forty years systematically investigating children who claimed memories of previous lives, developing the methodological standards that made this field of research scientifically credible. His approach required that children's statements be documented in full before any attempt at verification, and that investigation be conducted independently of the families involved. He collected over three thousand cases. His successor at the University of Virginia's Division of Perceptual Studies, Jim Tucker, has continued and expanded his work. Stevenson's body of research represents the most rigorous scientific investigation of reincarnation evidence ever conducted.

Stigmata

Wounds corresponding to the crucifixion wounds of Jesus Christ that appear on the hands, feet, and sometimes side of a person without apparent physical cause. The word comes from the Greek stigma, meaning mark or brand. The most extensively documented modern case is that of Padre Pio, who bore the stigmata on his hands and feet for fifty years from 1918 until his death in 1968, under repeated investigation by physicians, skeptics, and the Vatican.

Stone tape theory

A popular idea in paranormal investigation circles suggesting that anomalous phenomena are recordings imprinted in building materials and played back under certain conditions, similar to a magnetic tape. It is important to understand where this idea actually comes from. The concept originated not in scientific research but in a 1972 BBC television drama written by playwright Nigel Kneale, who created it deliberately as a fictional dramatic device and never intended it as a genuine explanatory framework. Kneale was a writer of considerable imagination and intellectual honesty, and he would likely have been dismayed to see his storytelling device treated as investigative theory. The author rejects it on evidentiary grounds: it does not account for why phenomena are perceptible only to sensitive individuals, why some phenomena respond interactively to observers rather than simply replaying, or why phenomena diminish over time. The Temporal Overlap Hypothesis offered in this book addresses those gaps in ways the stone tape concept never could.

Sufi / Sufism

The mystical dimension of Islam, focused on direct personal experience of the divine rather than doctrinal observance or external ritual. Sufism seeks the dissolution of the apparent boundary between the individual soul and God through practices including meditation, devotional music, movement, and contemplative prayer. Rumi was among the greatest voices of the Sufi tradition. Like mystical traditions in every major religion, Sufism arrives at the recognition that the individual and the whole are not ultimately separate.

Tarot

A deck of seventy-eight illustrated cards used for divination, reflection, and spiritual guidance. Tarot originated in fifteenth-century Europe as playing cards and evolved into a divinatory tool by the late eighteenth century. Like other divination instruments, tarot functions as a focusing mechanism for the practitioner's intuitive and psychic attention rather than as an independent source of information. The specific imagery on the cards gives the mind something concrete to work with while the underlying perception does the actual work.

Temporal Overlap Hypothesis

The author's own speculative framework for understanding residual anomalous phenomena, offered as a replacement for the scientifically baseless stone tape theory. The hypothesis proposes two components: that events of extreme emotional intensity may produce changes in the local field of a location that persist independently of any living observer (environmental embedding), and that these embedded impressions require interaction with a sufficiently sensitive living awareness to become perceptible (sensitive activation). The hypothesis generates specific testable predictions and is explicitly identified as speculative rather than proven.

Thought form

An entity or presence generated by sustained focused human attention and emotion rather than by an independent spiritual intelligence. Traditions including Tibetan Buddhism, where such constructs are called tulpas, acknowledge the capacity of directed consciousness to create something that takes on apparent life of its own. The author applies this concept to the Annabelle case, arguing that what gathered around the doll was built piece by piece from the focused attention of the nursing students who owned it rather than descending from some external darkness.

Tulpa

A concept from Tibetan Buddhist tradition referring to a being or object created through focused spiritual or mental discipline. A tulpa is understood as a manifestation of mind, brought into apparent existence through sustained concentrated intention. The concept has been adopted more broadly to describe any entity or phenomenon apparently generated by focused human awareness rather than by an external intelligence. Related to what the author calls a thought form.

Tucker, Jim

A psychiatrist and researcher at the University of Virginia's Division of

Perceptual Studies and the successor to Ian Stevenson in the investigation of children who claim to remember previous lives. Tucker has continued and expanded Stevenson's methodology, documenting thousands of cases in which children provide specific verifiable statements about past lives that prove accurate upon investigation. His work is cited in this book as among the strongest available evidence for the persistence of consciousness across lifetimes.

Umbanda

An Afro-Brazilian religion that emerged in Brazil in the early twentieth century, drawing on Yoruba spiritual traditions, Kardecism, Catholicism, and indigenous Brazilian practices. Umbanda centers on communication with a diverse range of spiritual entities through mediumship and possession trance, with the goal of healing and service. Every priest and priestess in Umbanda is trained to become a medium. The tradition treats spiritual sensitivity not as a rare calling but as a universal capacity to be developed responsibly within a community structure.

University of Virginia Division of Perceptual Studies

An academic research unit at the University of Virginia founded by psychiatrist Ian Stevenson, dedicated to the scientific investigation of phenomena suggesting survival of consciousness after death, including near-death experiences, apparitions, and the memories of young children who claim to recall previous lives. The division applies rigorous evidentiary standards, documenting children's specific statements before any attempt at verification and investigating independently. Its work represents the most extensive and methodologically careful body of research in this field.

Van Lommel, Pim

A Dutch cardiologist at Rijnstate Hospital who conducted the largest prospective study of near-death experiences in cardiac arrest survivors, published in The Lancet in 2001. His study documented cases of verified accurate perception during cardiac arrest with confirmed flat EEG and concluded that current scientific understanding cannot account for these experiences. He proposed that the brain functions as a receiver rather than a generator of consciousness. His work is among the most scientifically rigorous evidence for the hypothesis that awareness can function independently of brain activity.

Vedanta

One of the major schools of Hindu philosophy, based on the Upanishads, the Bhagavad Gita, and the Brahma Sutras. Advaita Vedanta, the non-dual school, holds that there is ultimately only one reality, Brahman, and that the individual self, the Atman, is identical to it. The experience of being a separate self is understood as Maya, or illusion, and liberation consists in the direct recognition of this non-duality. Advaita Vedanta is one of the most developed and rigorous philosophical expressions of the insight at the center of this book.

Warren, Ed

One of America's most prominent paranormal investigators, born in 1926 and active until his death in 2006. Ed Warren worked alongside his wife Lorraine for decades investigating hauntings, possessions, and other anomalous phenomena, including the Amityville case, the Annabelle case, and hundreds of others. He and Lorraine founded the New England Society for Psychic Research. Ed began investigating after a childhood encounter with the apparition of a deceased aunt, described in accurate verifiable detail. The author is his grandson.

Warren, Lorraine

One of America's most prominent psychics and paranormal investigators, born in 1927 and active until her death in 2019. Lorraine Warren worked alongside her husband Ed for decades and was widely considered one of the most gifted psychics of her generation. The author is her grandson and co-founded the Warren Legacy Foundation with her in 2013. He was present at her death and describes the moment, after months of Alzheimer's-related silence, when she looked at him with full recognition and told him she loved him.

Yechidah

In Kabbalistic teaching, the highest aspect of the soul, the level of selfhood most directly connected to the divine source. The word comes from the Hebrew for unity or oneness. At the level of Yechidah, the distinction between the individual and God dissolves. It is the Kabbalistic equivalent of what Hindu Vedanta calls the Atman recognized as identical to Brahman, what Christian mystics describe as the divine spark within, and what Rumi described as the ocean in the drop.

XXI. BIBLIOGRAPHY

The following works are cited, referenced, or drawn upon throughout The Warren Legacy, the Public Thesis, and the Academic Working Paper. Entries are organized by category and arranged alphabetically by author within each section.

NEAR-DEATH EXPERIENCE AND CONSCIOUSNESS RESEARCH

Alexander, Eben. Proof of Heaven: A Neurosurgeon's Journey into the Afterlife. Simon and Schuster, 2012.

Greyson, Bruce. After: A Doctor Explores What Near-Death Experiences Reveal About Life and Beyond. St. Martin's Essentials, 2021.

Moody, Raymond A. Life After Life: The Investigation of a Phenomenon-Survival of Bodily Death. Mockingbird Books, 1975.

Ring, Kenneth. Life at Death: A Scientific Investigation of the Near-Death Experience. Coward, McCann and Geoghegan, 1980.

Ring, Kenneth. Heading Toward Omega: In Search of the Meaning of the Near-Death Experience. William Morrow, 1984.

Ring, Kenneth, and Sharon Cooper. Mindsight: Near-Death and Out-of-Body Experiences in the Blind. William James Center for Consciousness Studies, 1999.

Van Lommel, Pim. Consciousness Beyond Life: The Science of the Near-Death Experience. HarperOne, 2010.

Van Lommel, Pim, Ruud van Wees, Vincent Meyers, and Ingrid Elfferich. "Near-Death Experience in Survivors of Cardiac Arrest: A Prospective Study in the Netherlands." The Lancet 358, no. 9298 (2001): 2039-2045.

CONSCIOUSNESS STUDIES AND PHILOSOPHY OF MIND

Goff, Philip. Galileo's Error: Foundations for a New Science of Mind. Pantheon Books, 2019.

Goff, Philip. Why? The Purpose of the Universe. Oxford University Press, 2023.

Hameroff, Stuart, and Roger Penrose. Consciousness in the Universe: A Review of the "Orch OR" Theory. Physics of Life Reviews 11, no. 1 (2014): 39-78.

Penrose, Roger. The Emperor's New Mind: Concerning Computers, Minds, and the Laws of Physics. Oxford University Press, 1989.

Penrose, Roger. Shadows of the Mind: A Search for the Missing Science of Consciousness. Oxford University Press, 1994.

PARAPSYCHOLOGY AND ANOMALOUS EXPERIENCE RESEARCH

Bancel, Peter A. Searching for Global Consciousness: A 17-Year Exploration. Explore: The Journal of Science and Healing 13, no. 2 (2017): 94-101.

Bem, Daryl J. Feeling the Future: Experimental Evidence for Anomalous Retroactive Influences on Cognition and Affect. Journal of Personality and Social Psychology 100, no. 3 (2011): 407-425.

Byrd, Randolph C. Positive Therapeutic Effects of Intercessory Prayer in a Coronary Care Unit Population. Southern Medical Journal 81, no. 7 (1988): 826-829.

Fach, Wolfgang, Anuschka Erhard-Weiss, Katrin Hansmann-Wiest, and Harald Walach. Exceptional Experiences (ExE) in Clinical Psychology: Findings from a Specialized Consultation Service. Frontiers in Psychology 4 (2013): 65.

Fisher, Matthew P. A. Quantum Cognition: The Possibility of Processing with Nuclear Spins in the Brain. Annals of Physics 362 (2015): 593-602.

Mossbridge, Julia A., Patrizio Tressoldi, and Jessica Utts. Predictive Physiological Anticipation Preceding Seemingly Unpredictable Stimuli: A Meta-Analysis. Frontiers in Psychology 3 (2012): 390.

Owen, A. R. G. Conjuring Up Philip: An Adventure in Psychokinesis. Harper and Row, 1976.

Price, Huw. Does Time-Symmetry Imply Retrocausality? How the Quantum World Says Maybe. Studies in History and Philosophy of Science Part B 43, no. 2 (2012): 75-83.

Radin, Dean. The Conscious Universe: The Scientific Truth of Psychic Phenomena. HarperEdge, 1997.

Radin, Dean. Entangled Minds: Extrasensory Experiences in a Quantum Reality. Paraview Pocket Books, 2006.

Stevenson, Ian. Twenty Cases Suggestive of Reincarnation. 2nd ed. University of Virginia Press, 1974.

Stevenson, Ian. Children Who Remember Previous Lives: A Question of Reincarnation. University Press of Virginia, 1987.

Tucker, Jim B. Life Before Life: A Scientific Investigation of Children's Memories of Previous Lives. St. Martin's Press, 2005.

Tucker, Jim B. Return to Life: Extraordinary Cases of Children Who Remember Past Lives. St. Martin's Press, 2013.

QUANTUM PHYSICS AND THEORETICAL FRAMEWORKS

Bohm, David. Wholeness and the Implicate Order. Routledge, 1980.

Price, Huw, and Ken Wharton. Disentangling the Quantum World. Entropy 17, no. 11 (2015): 7752-7767.

Zurek, Wojciech H. Decoherence, Einselection, and the Quantum Origins of the Classical. Reviews of Modern Physics 75, no. 3 (2003): 715-775.

NEUROSCIENCE, BIOLOGY, AND HUMAN PERCEPTION

Benson, Herbert, John W. Lehmann, M. S. Malhotra, Ralph F. Goldman, Jeffrey Hopkins, and Mark D. Epstein. Body Temperature Changes During the Practice of g-Tummo Yoga. Nature 295 (1982): 234-236.

Benson, Herbert, Jeffery A. Dusek, Jane B. Sherwood, Peter Lam, Charles F. Bethea, William Carpenter, Sidney Levitsky, et al. Study of the Therapeutic Effects of Intercessory Prayer (STEP) in Cardiac Bypass Patients. American Heart Journal 151, no. 4 (2006): 762-764.

Huels, Ethan R., UnCheol Lee, Adeola Shafiei Fard, Patrick Gulick, Steven Noh, Dajung Judy Kim, Zirui Huang, Georg Northoff, and Anthony G. Hudetz. Neural Correlates of the Shamanic State of Consciousness. Frontiers in Human Neuroscience 15 (2021): 610466.

Wang, Connie X., Isaac A. Hilburn, Daw-An Wu, Yuki Mizuhara, Christopher P. Cousins, Nathan M. Abramson, Shinsuke Shimojo, and Joseph L. Kirschvink. Transduction of the Geomagnetic Field as Evidenced from Alpha-Band Activity in the Human Brain. eNeuro 6, no. 2 (2019).

ARCHAEOLOGY AND CULTURAL TRANSMISSION

David, Bruno, Fiona Petchey, Jean-Jacques Delannoy, Joanna Freslov, Meredith Clark, Kelsey Lowe, Samuel Harper, et al. A 12,000-Year Unbroken Aboriginal Australian Tradition Identified by GWAS and Oral History. Nature Human Behaviour (2024). DOI: 10.1038/s41562-024-01912-w.

PSYCHOLOGY AND HUMAN DEVELOPMENT

Tedeschi, Richard G., and Lawrence G. Calhoun. Posttraumatic Growth: Conceptual Foundations and Empirical Evidence. Psychological Inquiry 15, no. 1 (2004): 1-18

Tedeschi, Richard G., and Lawrence G. Calhoun. Trauma and Transformation: Growing in the Aftermath of Suffering. Sage Publications, 1995.

PHILOSOPHY AND HISTORY OF SCIENCE

Kuhn, Thomas S. The Structure of Scientific Revolutions. University of Chicago Press, 1962.

Parmenides of Elea. On Nature. Circa 475 BCE. Translated fragments widely available in: McKirahan, Richard D. Philosophy Before Socrates. Hackett Publishing, 1994.

SPIRITUAL TRADITIONS AND COMPARATIVE RELIGION

Eliade, Mircea. Shamanism: Archaic Techniques of Ecstasy. Translated by Willard R. Trask. Pantheon Books, 1964.

James, William. The Varieties of Religious Experience: A Study in Human Nature. Longmans, Green, and Co., 1902.

Kardec, Allan. The Spirit's Book. Translated by Anna Blackwell. Livraria EspÃ-rita Allan Kardec, 1857. Reprint, International Spiritist Council, 2010.

Neihardt, John G. Black Elk Speaks: Being the Life Story of a Holy Man of the Oglala Sioux. William Morrow, 1932.

Rumi, Jalal ad-Din Muhammad. The Essential Rumi. Translated by Coleman Barks with John Moyne. HarperOne, 1995.

Sheldrake, Rupert. Morphic Resonance: The Nature of Formative Causation. Park Street Press, 2009.

Sheldrake, Rupert. The Science Delusion: Freeing the Spirit of Enquiry. Coronet, 2012. Published in the United States as Science Set Free. Deepak Chopra Books, 2012.

PARANORMAL INVESTIGATION AND CASE STUDIES

Brittle, Gerald. The Demonologist: The Extraordinary Career of Ed and Lorraine Warren. Prentice-Hall, 1980.

Warren, Ed, and Lorraine Warren, with Robert David Chase. Ghost Hunters: True Stories from the World's Most Famous Demonologists. St. Martin's Paperbacks, 1989.

Warren, Ed, and Lorraine Warren, with Robert David Chase. Graveyard: True Hauntings from an Old New England Cemetery. St. Martin's Paperbacks, 1992.

LITERATURE

Bach, Richard. Illusions: The Adventures of a Reluctant Messiah. Delacorte Press, 1977.

Shelley, Percy Bysshe. Ozymandias. First published in The Examiner, January 11, 1818.

ABOUT THE AUTHOR

Chris McKinnell began this work at sixteen years old in a darkened room in Lee, Massachusetts, because his grandfather trusted him enough to walk him into it.

Forty-four years and more than ten thousand cases later, he is still asking the same questions that room first raised. As co-founder and Director of the Warren Legacy Foundation for Paranormal Research, which he established with Lorraine Warren in 2013, Chris has investigated across six continents, sitting with Animist communities in Mali, Umbanda priests in Portugal, Buddhist monks in Thailand, and families in crisis in living rooms across North America and Europe.

He led several of the investigations his grandparents are best known for, including the Snedeker haunting in Connecticut, where he lived in the house for nine and a half weeks, and the Maurice Thériault exorcism. He does not charge for his work. He never has.

Chris has been featured in People, Esquire, and TMZ, and has appeared on the History Channel. He is currently in development for a television series exploring how cultures around the world manifest, understand, and live with the paranormal.

He lectures internationally and can be reached at chrismckinnell.com.